Also by Emeril Lagasse

EMERIL'S CREOLE CHRISTMAS

EMERIL'S DELMONICO: A RESTAURANT WITH A PAST

EMERIL'S NEW NEW ORLEANS COOKING

EMERIL'S POTLUCK: COMFORT FOOD WITH A KICKED-UP ATTITUDE

EMERIL'S THERE'S A CHEF IN MY SOUP!: RECIPES FOR THE KID IN EVERYONE

EMERIL'S THERE'S A CHEF IN MY FAMILY!: RECIPES TO GET EVERYBODY COOKING

EMERIL'S THERE'S A CHEF IN MY WORLD!: RECIPES THAT TAKE YOU PLACES

EMERIL'S TV DINNERS: KICKIN' IT UP A NOTCH
WITH RECIPES FROM EMERIL LIVE AND ESSENCE OF EMERIL

EVERY DAY'S A PARTY: LOUISIANA RECIPES
FOR CELEBRATING WITH FAMILY AND FRIENDS

FROM EMERIL'S KITCHENS: FAVORITE RECIPES FROM EMERIL'S RESTAURANTS

LOUISIANA REAL AND RUSTIC

PRIME TIME EMERIL: MORE TV DINNERS FROM AMERICA'S FAVORITE CHEF

Emeril
at the Grill

A COOKBOOK FOR ALL SEASONS

Emeril Lagasse

with Photography by Steven Freeman

An Imprint of HarperCollins*Publishers*

HarperCollins books may be purchased for educational, business, or sales promotional use. For information please write: Special Markets Department, HarperCollins Publishers, 10 East 53rd Street, New York, NY 10022.

FIRST EDITION

Designed by Leah Carlson-Stanisic

Library of Congress Cataloging-in-Publication Data has been applied for.

ISBN 978-0-06-174274-3

09 10 11 12 13 ID/RRD 10 9 8 7 6 5 4 3 2 1

I'd like to dedicate this book to my dad,
Emeril John Lagasse Jr., better known as
Mr. John. To my pal, with love:
may you grill forever.

And, of course, to my wife, Alden, and all of
my children: may we keep grilling together!

Acknowledgments

Many, many people have contributed to the fun and the creation of this amazing book. Let's face it, grilling indoors or outdoors is always fun and benefits from having many helping hands onboard. My thanks go out to all of you!

My loving and supportive family

My wife, Alden. My children, Jessie, Jillian, EJ, and Meril. Mom and Dad. My brother, Mark, and my sister-in-law, Wendi, and their daughter, Katie Bug. Sister Deloris and her son, Jason, and last but not least, our new grandbaby, Jude.

The Emeril's Homebase culinary team

Charlotte Martory for her amazing vision and talents, and for the talents of Alain Joseph, Stacey Meyer, Angela Sagabaen, and Kamili Hemphill. Thank you.

The amazing team at Emeril's Homebase

Eric Linquest, Tony Cruz, Dave McCelvey, Marti Dalton, Chef Chris Wilson, Chef Bernard Carmouche, Chef Dana D'Anzi, Tony Lott, Scott Farber, Doug Doran, George Ditta. Thank you for all of your support and friendship.

The Steven Freeman photography team

Wow! Such photo-capturing moments!

Steven Freeman

Kevin Guiler

Josh Maready

The Martha Stewart team

Martha Stewart, for her creativity and dedication. Charles Koppleman, for being such a great chairman. Robin Marino and Wenda Harris Millard, co-CEOs, for their friendship and leadership. Leslie Stockton and the entire test kitchen staff, especially Gabe, Elizabeth, and Miss Geri.

Special thanks to Lucinda Scala Quinn for her special vision and touch.

My Super M's

Mara Warner Jones

Michelle Terrebonne

Maggie McCabe

Special thanks to Mimi Rice for her amazing eyes and constant photo editing. Also, where would we have been without TJ Pitre, whose technical assistance made the whole shoot come together.

Style team

Jed Holtz—our awesome prop designer

Charissa Melnik—our wonderful culinary stylist

Shelley Van Gage

Our partners at HarperStudio

Bob Miller, Debbie Stier, Sarah Burningham, Julia Cheiffetz, Katie Salisbury, Mary Schuck, Leah Carlson-Stanisic, Kim Lewis, Lorie Young, Nikki Cutler, Doug Jones, Kathie Ness, Ann Cahn

· · · · · · · · · · · · · · · · ·

Our wonderful partners at All-Clad, T-Fal, Weber, and Wusthof.

My friends and amazing purveyors at Leonard Simchick Prime Meats and Fresh Poultry and Pisacane Fish Market.

The hardworking staff at each of my restaurants—Emeril's New Orleans, NOLA, Emeril's Delmonico, Emeril's New Orleans Fish House, Delmonico Steakhouse, Emeril's Orlando, Tchoup Chop, Emeril's Miami Beach, Emeril's Gulf Coast Fish House, and Table 10.

All the great, hardworking people at Homebase that make it all happen.

My good friends, Frank and Richard Santorsola.

My man, Sherif—you're always there and you're always on time.

My agent and friend, Jim Griffin.

My trusted friend and lawyer of twenty years, Mark Stein.

And last but not least, where would I be without Tony Cruz, my dear friend and business partner. Special, special thanks to him and his wife, Lizzy, and their daughter, Mallory, for their friendship, love, and support.

contents

SANDWICHES, WRAPS, AND PIZZAS

BURGERS AND KEBABS

FROM THE SEA

THINGS WITH WINGS

OFF THE LAND

SWEET ENDINGS

Introduction

Oh, yeah, babe. What can I say? You know, growing up in Fall River with my dad, Mr. John, at the head of every grilling opportunity really paved the way for my love of the grill. It didn't matter if it was Dad's day off from work, or if he and my mom, Hilda, were having a family gathering at the house, or even if it was one of those beach cookouts that we all loved, digging for clams and swimming and just having a fun, laid-back time with the family. There is something about the grilling experience that just meant good times for me from an early age. Dad would shop and set up the party, Mom would be in the kitchen, cooking up the sides, and then, when the time was right, they'd light the fire and share a beer as the coals got nice and hot. Let me tell you, folks, this was definitely not just about hot dogs and hamburgers!

So when I sat down to get started on this book, the memories just came flooding in. Many of the recipes included here are inspired from those family times, and many have come from friends and experiences along the way. The common theme is that they are simple, fun, approachable, and incredibly tasty and delicious—and that there is something for everyone, for every season. Since my family loves to grill year-round, I've tried to give tips on how many of these recipes work great on indoor grills when the weather isn't so inviting. Because let's face it: when the grill calls, you've just gotta make it happen!

After years of seeing friends sweat when faced with a grilling challenge, I've come to realize that many of us must feel a little intimidated by the grill—maybe it's a lack of understanding about how to control the temperature, or how long to cook something, or how to get those coals just where you want 'em—whether it's a gas grill outside or an electric grill indoors. Let me tell you, it's really pretty simple. Understand this: The grill is its own animal, and experience is the only key to making it work for you. The more you do it, the more you "get" it. So I invite you, my friends, to grill along with me. Get yourself a good thermometer, learn how to control the heat, practice good food safety techniques by handling uncooked foods properly and always using clean utensils with cooked foods—just get comfortable with your grill and I promise you, you will be rewarded with good times and great food.

On a final note, it is my feeling that one of the most important but often overlooked elements of good grilling is using the best possible ingredients, preferably local and seasonal. Whether it's meat, chicken, fish, veggies, whatever—it should be fresh, fresh, fresh. Great ingredients and simple grilling techniques just go together; that's how it is. The good news is that this is one element of grilling that *is* easy. Get to know your local farmers. Go to the farmers' market often to buy fresh produce, meats, and seafood. With fresh, quality ingredients to begin with, you're well on your way to grilling success. In the end, it really doesn't matter if you're on the beach, at the ballpark with the kids, or at a family gathering in your backyard. Keep it simple, keep it fresh, remember that practice makes perfect, and above everything else, make sure to remember that grilling is one of the great American pastimes. Be proud of being one who loves to grill.

EMERIL J. LAGASSE III

TOOLS AND TECHNIQUES

Tools That Come in Handy

GRILL/WIRE BRUSH: An essential tool to have when cleaning your grill. Having clean grates helps prevent food from sticking.

TONGS: These are useful for turning foods on the grill—especially the long-handled variety to protect your arms from the heat. Having several pairs on hand is helpful for handling raw and cooked foods separately.

BASTING BRUSH: Any basting or food-safe brush will do, but it's best to choose a brush with natural bristles since they hold up to the heat better.

SPATULA: A long-handled metal spatula is key for turning foods like grilled vegetables, burgers, and whole fish.

SKEWERS: Making kebabs is fun, and kids love to participate. Wooden skewers are inexpensive and easy to find but must always be soaked before using (and sometimes will still burn if on the grill for a long time). Metal skewers are reusable and will last forever. Skewers can also be made of unique, fun items like rosemary stems and sugar-cane swizzle sticks.

PLASTIC SPRAY BOTTLE: Fill a bottle with water so you can easily put out flare-ups on the grill, but take care not to overspray or you will end up with ashes everywhere!

OLD RAGS: Use these to oil down your grates without having to worry about ruining nice towels. Just be sure they are clean and free of any chemicals.

MEAT THERMOMETER (PREFERABLY INSTANT-READ): Make this tool your best friend because you want to rely more on your thermometer than on any specified cooking time. This will give you a more accurate gauge as to when your food is done. Make sure to purchase one that is housed in a heat-resistant casing—plastic versions simply can't stand up to the heat!

Gas vs. Charcoal: Some Thoughts

When you are choosing a grill, think about your needs and desires. Do you plan on cooking for a crowd? How often will you grill? How much space do you have in your backyard? What is your lifestyle like? Do you have the time necessary to wait for embers to grow hot? How much do you want to spend? Do you want to transport your grill? These are all questions one needs to contemplate before making the final decision.

. . . .

✦ Many Americans today opt for a gas grill, mainly for the convenience. Gas grills are easier to clean, stay hot for much longer periods of time without your having to worry about adding more coals or wood, and can inspire people to get out and grill at all times of the year. They may also offer more versatility and accessory options: for example, some come with side burners, infrared burners, and/or a rotisserie.

. . . .

✦ Also, with gas grills all you have to do is ignite the flame and there you go, you are on your way to a backyard barbecue. Just let the grill heat up to the desired temperature, and then start cooking. It's also easier to control the grilling temperature.

. . . .

✦ Some die-hard barbecue enthusiasts say that grilling over a live flame of hardwood charcoal is the only way to go. You capture more of the char flavor in your foods and it is a more "hands-on" experience. You can get a great sear from the high heat or can cook at low temperatures for "low and slow" cooking. Add some wood chunks and it doubles as a smoker! Charcoal grills tend to be more easily transportable, too.

. . . .

Types of Charcoal and Wood

I prefer hardwood to charcoal for several reasons. It burns cleaner and hotter, and it permeates your food with wood flavor rather than with the flavor of chemicals that you can get from a lot of household charcoals. By the way, I try to avoid using lighter fluid if at all possible; it can really detract from the flavor of your food and sometimes leaves foods with an unappealing aftertaste.

Getting That Fire Started!

The simplest way to light a hardwood or charcoal fire is to either build a pyramid with your coals or to use a metal cylinder, called a chimney. To get the fire started, stuff a bit of newspaper at the bottom of your chimney or pyramid, open the bottom vent holes in the grill, and light the paper from the bottom of the grill. The paper will ignite the coals. Once all of the coals are lit and hot (beginning to turn gray), they can be poured out onto the bottom grill grate. Place the upper grate on the grill, above the hot charcoal. Control the heat by moving the coals around, allowing you to cook with both direct and indirect heat, as desired.

Smokin'

When I want to kick it up, I like to add hardwood chips or chunks to the grill; it adds bold smoky flavors. The most common woods used for chips or chunks are hickory and mesquite, but you can also find alder, apple, cherry, and my personal favorite, pecan. Each type of wood lends a different flavor; it can be fun to experiment so you can decide what works best for you. Wood chips and chunks should be soaked in water for at least 30 minutes before they are ready to use. If you are grilling over charcoal, heat the coals and then scatter your chips or chunks over them. When using a gas grill, you can use a smoker attachment if it allows for one. If not, there are various ways to improvise. We suggest wrapping chips/chunks in an aluminum foil pouch (poked with holes so that smoke can escape) and placing this pouch directly onto the burner unit.

Cooking with Common Sense

The main thing to keep in mind about grilling is that every grill is a little different. In this book I give specific cooking times in the recipes, but you need to use your noggin. Be attentive: if your grill burns hotter than mine, your cooking time may be different. If you are grilling outside on a cold and windy day, your grill may not get as hot and your food will likely take a little longer to cook. You need to trust yourself (and your thermometer). Use good judgment. And before you know it, grilling will become second nature.

Grill Maintenance

One of the most important but least exciting things to think about when grilling is how to keep your grill clean. Every time you use your grill, heat it up, covered, for 15 to 20 minutes, and then use a grill brush to brush the grates clean before grilling. The beauty about using this method is that any leftover bits from the previous use will be burned off and then easily brushed away.

If you use your grill regularly, take the time every now and again to give the grill a good thorough cleaning.

· ·

✦ If you have a gas grill, not only should you brush the grates on all sides to thoroughly clean them, but you should also remove any ash and debris that have gathered on the V-shaped grates below the grill grates. This will help reduce any flare-ups and will prolong the life of your grill. Finally, make sure to remove all of the debris and grease that have built up in the collection tray. Every once in a while it is good to wash the whole thing down with a little mild soapy water.

· ·

✦ For charcoal grills, maintenance is pretty much the same. However, it is also important that you regularly dispose of any leftover ash that gathers in the bottom of the grill. If it is left for any length of time, it can cause your grill to rust.

· ·

Emeril *at the* Grill

TO "WET" THE Appetite

CAIPIRINHA

Growing up in Fall River, Massachussetts, a predominantly Portuguese community, I learned that cachaça to the Portuguese is like grappa to the Italians: something to enjoy daily! I think you'll find that in the warm-weather months, this lime and cachaça experience is a great refreshing way to kick off an outdoor eating event.

3 limes

1/2 cup sugar

1 1/2 quarts ice cubes

1 cup cachaça (Brazilian brandy made from sugarcane)

Lime slices or sugarcane swizzle sticks, for garnish (optional)

1. Cut each lime in half crosswise, then cut each half into 8 pieces. Place 12 pieces of lime in each of four double old-fashioned glasses (or other 12-ounce glasses). Sprinkle 2 tablespoons of the sugar into each glass. Using a muddler (or the butt end of a large wooden spoon), mash the limes into the bottom of the glass until the sugar is dissolved, stirring occasionally. Fill each glass with 1 1/2 cups of the ice and 1/4 cup of the cachaça. One glass at a time, transfer the contents of the glass to a cocktail shaker, and invert the glass over the shaker to act as a lid. Shake the glass and shaker together to combine the sugar and cachaça, shaking until well chilled. Lift the glass from the shaker, and pour the contents back into the glass. Repeat the process with the remaining three glasses.

2. Garnish with a slice of lime or a sugarcane swizzle stick, if desired.

4 servings

ROSÉ SANGRÍA

If you're a fan of sangría, check out this version made with rosé wine. It's especially nice served ice-cold on a hot summer day, and it couldn't be easier to make.

Two 750ml bottles rosé wine

½ cup Spanish brandy

¼ cup Spanish orange liqueur, Grand Marnier, or Triple Sec

Juice of 1 orange

½ cup superfine sugar

½ cup sliced fresh strawberries

½ orange, sliced into thin rounds, cut in half

½ lemon, sliced into thin rounds, cut in half

½ plum, pit removed, sliced into thin wedges

½ peach, pit removed, sliced into thin wedges

One 10-ounce bottle club soda, chilled

Ice cubes, for serving (optional)

1. Combine the wine, brandy, orange liqueur, orange juice, and sugar in a large pitcher and stir until the sugar has dissolved. Add the remaining fruit and stir well to combine. Cover and refrigerate until well chilled, about 2 hours.

2. Stir in the club soda and serve the sangría in large wineglasses, over ice if desired.

10 to 12 servings

PIÑA COLADA MOJITO

Another refreshing libation to keep your grilling party going strong. Don't skimp on the flavored rums here—they're what make this drink special.

. . . .

¼ lime, cut into 4 pieces

8 fresh mint leaves

2 teaspoons natural raw cane sugar

1 cup crushed or chipped ice

1 tablespoon Mint Syrup
    (recipe follows)

1 tablespoon unsweetened
    coconut milk

1 tablespoon pineapple juice

2 tablespoons
    pineapple-flavored rum

2 tablespoons
    coconut-flavored rum

Splash of seltzer water

Sugarcane sticks, for garnish

Fresh mint leaves, for garnish

Place the lime pieces in a 12-ounce glass, and top them with the mint leaves and cane sugar. Using a muddler, crush the lime pieces while bruising the mint with the sugar. Fill the glass to just below the rim with the ice. Add the mint syrup, coconut milk, pineapple juice, pineapple rum, and coconut rum. Transfer the contents of the glass to a cocktail shaker, and invert the glass over the shaker to act as a lid. Vigorously shake the glass and shaker together for at least 30 seconds. Pour the mojito back into the glass and top it off with the seltzer water. Place a sugarcane stick in the glass, garnish with fresh mint leaves, and serve immediately.

1 serving

Mint Syrup

2 cups sugar
1 cup water
1 cup packed fresh mint leaves

1. Combine the sugar and water in a small saucepan. Bring to a gentle boil over medium-low heat, stirring occasionally to help dissolve the sugar. While the syrup heats, rinse the mint leaves to eliminate any dirt. Once the sugar has dissolved, remove the syrup from the heat and add the mint leaves. Allow the syrup to cool for at least 1 hour before straining out the mint.

2. Store the syrup in an airtight container in the refrigerator until ready to use. The syrup will keep, refrigerated, for several weeks. **2 cups**

MANGO-CITRUS DAIQUIRI

Mangoes and limes are best friends. Add rum and ice, and this refreshing spin on the traditional daiquiri will make your friends happy, happy, happy!

3/4 cup freshly squeezed
    lime juice

1/2 cup sugar

One 16-ounce package frozen
    mango cubes

2/3 cup Bacardi Limon rum

1/3 cup Cointreau

4 cups ice cubes

1 lime wedge (optional)

Superfine sugar, for coating glass
    rims (optional)

4 to 6 lime slices,
    for garnish

1. Combine the lime juice, sugar, mango cubes, rum, Cointreau, and ice in a blender and process on high speed until completely smooth, 2 to 3 minutes.

2. Rub the rims of four to six stemmed glasses with the lime wedge. Then dip each glass in the superfine sugar to coat the rim, if desired.

3. Pour the daiquiri into the prepared glasses, and garnish each with a lime slice.

4 to 6 servings

WATERMELON MARGARITAS

I suggest making this mellow, less tart version of a margarita in the thick of summer, when watermelons are at their peak of goodness.

....

¹/₄ cup sugar

2 tablespoons water

¹/₂ teaspoon finely grated lime zest

3 cups seeded, cubed watermelon (2-inch pieces)

¹/₄ cup plus 2 tablespoons premium white tequila

¹/₄ cup Triple Sec

2 tablespoons freshly squeezed lime juice

2 tablespoons kosher salt

1 lime wedge

1 cup ice cubes

1. Combine the sugar, water, and lime zest in a small saucepan. Bring to a boil over medium heat, stirring until the sugar dissolves. Remove from the heat and cool to room temperature. (This lime syrup can be made ahead and kept in a covered container in the refrigerator for up to a week until ready to use.)

2. Chill two margarita glasses in the freezer for 30 minutes.

3. Place the watermelon in a blender and pulse until smooth. (You may need to stir the watermelon between pulses to facilitate pureeing.) Measure out 1¹/₂ cups of the watermelon puree in a large liquid measuring cup. Add the tequila, Triple Sec, lime juice, and 1 tablespoon of the cooled lime syrup to the puree.

4. Spread the kosher salt in a shallow dish. Wet the rim of the chilled margarita glasses with the lime wedge, and dip them, one at a time, into the salt, twisting to coat the rims.

5. Pour the ice into a cocktail shaker, add the watermelon-tequila mixture, and shake until frothy and well chilled. Strain into the prepared glasses, and serve immediately.

2 servings

PEACHY GINGER LEMONADE COCKTAIL

This concoction is light and refreshing—just the drink to make when peaches are in season. Any unused peach puree can be added to smoothies: just store it in a nonreactive airtight container in the fridge for up to 2 days, or freeze it in small amounts in an ice cube tray and take them out of the freezer as needed.

2 ripe peaches, peeled, pitted, and chopped

2 tablespoons minced fresh ginger

2 tablespoons freshly squeezed lemon juice

8 ounces lemonade

3 ounces orange-flavored vodka (optional)

Crushed ice

1. Combine the peaches, ginger, and lemon juice in a blender and puree until smooth.

2. Combine 2 tablespoons of the peach puree with the lemonade, vodka if using, and ice in a cocktail shaker, and shake well to combine. Strain the mixture over crushed ice in two tall glasses, and serve immediately.

2 servings

SUMMERY CITRUS, GINGER, AND RASPBERRY PUNCH

This punch is the perfect cool beverage to make for a crowd when you have a grilling get-together, and is equally delicious when made without the alcohol if children are attending the party.

1½ cups sugar

¾ cup water

½ cup thinly sliced fresh ginger

1 pint fresh raspberries

2 cups freshly squeezed orange juice

½ cup freshly squeezed lemon juice

½ cup freshly squeezed lime juice

3 cups dry gin, chilled

4 cups seltzer water, chilled

Ice cubes, for serving

1. Combine the sugar, water, and ginger in a 1-quart saucepan. Set the pan over medium heat and cook, stirring occasionally, until the sugar has dissolved, about 15 minutes. Allow the syrup to cool completely. Then strain it through a fine-mesh sieve into a container (discard the solids). Refrigerate the syrup until ready to use.

2. Place the raspberries in a food processor and process until pureed. Strain the raspberry puree through a fine-mesh strainer into a bowl, and set aside until ready to use. (Discard the seeds.)

3. In a 3-quart pitcher or a punch bowl, combine all the remaining ingredients with the raspberry puree and the syrup. Stir to combine, and serve over ice in small glasses or punch cups.

8 to 12 servings

MELON AND PINEAPPLE AGUA FRESCA

After Hurricane Katrina, a good number of Hispanic-Americans came to New Orleans to help rebuild the city. All of a sudden, taco trucks popped up everywhere. Talk about authentic! Talk about delicious! You can buy different versions of this drink straight from the trucks. It is very simple, but absolutely amazing. Fresh fruit of the day, a bit of sugar, and water—that's it! Here's my recipe.

1 cantaloupe, halved, seeded, peeled, and roughly chopped

3/4 to 1 cup sugar, to taste

5 cups water

1 cup diced fresh pineapple (small dice)

Ice cubes, for serving

Combine the cantaloupe and sugar in a blender and puree until smooth. Transfer the puree to a 3-quart pitcher, and add the water and pineapple. Stir well to combine, making sure that the sugar has completely dissolved. Serve in tall glasses filled with ice.

8 to 10 servings

LEMONY SPIKED SWEET TEA

Kicked up with golden rum, this sweet tea is an interesting take on a long-time Southern classic.

7 cups water

6 orange pekoe tea bags

1½ cups sugar

1⅓ cups freshly squeezed
   lemon juice

1 cup Bacardi 151 or other
   high-proof golden rum

Fresh mint sprigs,
   for garnish

1. Bring 4 cups of the water to a boil in a medium saucepan and add the tea bags. Remove the pan from the heat, cover it, and allow the tea bags to steep for 5 minutes.

2. Remove and discard the tea bags. Add the sugar to the saucepan and stir until dissolved. Add the remaining 3 cups water and stir to combine. Transfer the mixture to a pitcher, and add the lemon juice and rum. Chill thoroughly before serving.

3. Serve over ice, in tall glasses garnished with mint sprigs.

8 to 10 servings

GIN AND CUCUMBER COOLER

The combo of chilled gin and seeded cucumbers is incredibly surprising! We tested this drink using Hendrick's gin and talk about tasty . . . Oh, yeah, baby.

1 large cucumber (10 to 12 ounces), peeled, halved lengthwise, seeded, and cut into ¼-inch-thick half-moons

½ cup fresh cilantro leaves

1 quart crushed ice

¼ cup Cilantro Syrup (recipe follows)

¾ cup freshly squeezed ruby red grapefruit juice

1 cup gin

½ cup grapefruit soda (such as Blue Sky or Fresca)

Combine the cucumber and cilantro in a food processor and pulse until a chunky puree. Divide the puree among four 12-ounce glasses. Add 1 cup of the ice, 1 tablespoon of the cilantro syrup, 3 tablespoons of the grapefruit juice, and ¼ cup of the gin to each of the four glasses. One at a time, transfer the contents of each glass to a cocktail shaker, invert the glass over the shaker to act as a lid, and shake the glass and shaker together vigorously. Then return the cocktail to the glass, top it with 2 tablespoons of the grapefruit soda, and serve.

4 servings

Cilantro Syrup

1 cup sugar
½ cup water
1½ to 2 cups coarsely chopped cilantro (stems and leaves), rinsed and patted dry

Combine all the ingredients in a 1-quart saucepan, and bring to a boil, stirring occasionally to help dissolve the sugar. Once the mixture comes to a boil, remove the pan from the heat and let cool completely. Strain the cooled syrup through a fine-mesh sieve into a plastic container, and store in the refrigerator for up to 3 weeks. **1 cup**

ALMOND DREAM

This kid-friendly concoction will wow you with its rich flavor and will make kids (of all ages) feel truly special. For the best results, be sure to use a sugar-free, all-natural almond butter—available in health food stores and natural food stores.

1 pint premium nonfat vanilla frozen yogurt

½ cup almond milk

2 tablespoons almond butter

1 teaspoon vanilla extract

Place all the ingredients in a blender and process on low speed until they are well incorporated and a smooth shake forms, 30 to 45 seconds. Divide the shake evenly among four glasses, and serve immediately.

Note: For an extra-special treat, blend in ¾ cup crumbled cookies (such as chocolate sandwich cookies, chocolate chip cookies, or shortbread).

4 servings

ON THE
Side

GRILLED SMASHED POTATOES

Here's an out-of-the-ordinary way to use Red Bliss potatoes. I've also done this successfully with Yukon Gold potatoes. If you're not a rosemary fan, simply use an herb that you do love, such as cilantro or basil.

½ cup olive oil

2 tablespoons minced garlic

1½ teaspoons chopped fresh rosemary

2 pounds baby Red Bliss potatoes (no larger than 2 inches each), scrubbed well

1 teaspoon kosher salt

¼ teaspoon freshly ground coarse black pepper

1. Stir the olive oil, garlic, and rosemary together in a small bowl and let it sit at room temperature for at least 15 minutes for the flavors to infuse.

2. Preheat a grill to medium-high.

3. Place the potatoes in a pot of salted water and bring to a boil. Reduce the heat to a simmer and cook until the potatoes are tender when pierced with the tip of a knife, about 12 minutes. Drain the potatoes, discarding the water.

4. Using a towel wrapped around the palm of your hand, gently smash each potato until the skin breaks, while trying to keep the potato whole (leaving it about 1 inch thick). Transfer the potatoes to a baking sheet. Generously brush both sides of the potatoes with the olive oil mixture, and season both sides with the salt and pepper.

5. Place the potatoes on the grill and cook until grill marks appear and the potatoes are nicely caramelized, 3 to 4 minutes per side.

4 to 6 servings

SQUASH RIBBON SALAD WITH GOAT CHEESE

This simple salad is a great way to use the abundance of zucchini and yellow squash that is always found in your garden and farmers' markets near summer's end. The unusual, thin-cut ribbons absorb the simple vinaigrette, and the goat cheese adds an interesting saltiness and tang. If you have one, use a French or Japanese mandoline to cut the squash—it ensures uniform cuts and makes slicing a breeze.

1½ pounds small zucchini

1½ pounds small yellow squash

6 tablespoons white wine vinegar or champagne vinegar

½ cup extra-virgin olive oil

¾ teaspoon salt

½ teaspoon freshly ground black pepper, or to taste

½ cup julienned fresh mint

¼ cup julienned fresh basil

2 tablespoons minced fresh chives

6 ounces fresh goat cheese, crumbled

¼ cup pine nuts, lightly toasted

1. Bring a large pot of salted water to a boil. Add the zucchini and yellow squash and cook for 1½ minutes. Drain, and set aside to cool.

2. When the squash are cool enough to handle, slice them very thin lengthwise, using a mandoline or a sharp knife. Transfer the squash ribbons to a mixing bowl.

3. In a small bowl, combine the vinegar, olive oil, salt, and pepper.

4. When the squash has cooled completely, add the vinaigrette, mint, basil, and chives. Toss gently to combine. Crumble the goat cheese over the top, sprinkle with the pine nuts, and serve immediately.

8 servings

AVOCADO, TOMATO, AND RED ONION SALAD

This recipe brings it on home for me. A simple salad that pairs well with lots of dishes, this is especially good alongside the Grilled Marinated Flank Steak with Chimichurri Sauce on page 188.

2 Hass avocados, peeled, pitted, and cut into 8 slices each

1 pound Roma tomatoes, quartered

1/2 cup thinly sliced red onion

1/2 cup flat-leaf parsley leaves

Salt and freshly ground black pepper, to taste

3 tablespoons extra-virgin olive oil

1 tablespoon freshly squeezed lime juice

Arrange the avocados, tomatoes, onions, and parsley on a platter and season with the salt and pepper. Drizzle with the olive oil and lime juice, and serve immediately.

4 to 6 servings

SWEET AND TANGY COLESLAW

You can serve this simple coleslaw with just about any grilled meat or fish. It's a great salad to set out while the weather is warm because there's no mayo in it.

1⅓ cups sugar

1 cup white vinegar

2½ pounds cabbage, cored and shredded

2 cups finely chopped celery

3 medium carrots, shredded

1 green bell pepper, stemmed, seeded, and finely chopped

⅔ cup finely chopped onion

1 teaspoon celery seeds

1 teaspoon mustard seeds

Salt and freshly ground black pepper, to taste

Emeril's Original Essence or Creole Seasoning, to taste

1. Combine the sugar and vinegar in a small saucepan and heat, stirring occasionally, until the sugar has dissolved. Set aside to cool completely.

2. Assemble all the vegetables, the celery seeds, and the mustard seeds in a large nonreactive mixing bowl, and pour the cooled sugar-vinegar mixture over all. Toss well to combine, cover with plastic wrap, and refrigerate overnight.

3. When ready to serve, season the coleslaw with salt, freshly ground black pepper, and Essence to taste. Toss thoroughly to combine.

8 servings

Creole Seasoning

2½ tablespoons paprika
2 tablespoons salt
2 tablespoons garlic powder
1 tablespoon black pepper
1 tablespoon onion powder
1 tablespoon cayenne pepper
1 tablespoon dried oregano
1 tablespoon dried thyme

Combine all the ingredients thoroughly. **⅔ cup**

CHIPOTLE-DEVILED EGGS

I love deviled eggs. All kinds. But the heat of the chipotle—a smoked jala-peño that is available canned—really kicks this dish up. You can find canned chipotles in adobo sauce in the international section of most grocery stores.

12 hard-boiled large eggs, peeled

½ cup mayonnaise

2 tablespoons finely minced pickled jalapeños, drained

2 tablespoons finely chopped chipotle chile in adobo sauce

½ teaspoon Emeril's Southwest Essence spice blend

Pinch of salt, or more to taste

¼ teaspoon hot smoked paprika, such as Pimentón de la Vera, for garnish

1. Slice the eggs in half lengthwise and carefully remove the yolks. Set the whites aside. Press the yolks through a fine-mesh sieve into a mixing bowl. Add the mayonnaise, jalapeños, chipotle in adobo, Southwest Essence, and salt to taste. Stir to blend well. Spoon the mixture into the hollowed egg whites (or, alternatively, pipe with a pastry bag). Cover and refrigerate for at least 1 hour and up to overnight.

2. Just before serving, sprinkle the paprika over the deviled eggs. (If the paprika is added too early, it will stain the eggs.)

24 deviled eggs

SIMPLE CUCUMBER SALAD

Some foods need very little to enhance their flavor, and cucumbers happen to be one of them. A little salt, vinegar, and sugar is all they need. Check it out.

3 large seedless cucumbers (about 1 pound each), or 4 pounds regular cucumbers

1½ teaspoons salt

¼ cup white vinegar

¼ cup cider vinegar

½ cup sugar

1 tablespoon chopped fresh chives

1. Peel the cucumbers and cut them in half lengthwise. Using a small spoon or a melon baller, scoop out the seeds and watery center from each half, forming a shallow groove down the center.

2. Using a sharp paring knife, slice the cucumbers crosswise as thin as possible, ideally about ⅛ inch thick.

3. Place the cucumbers in a colander and sprinkle with the salt. Using clean hands, toss to combine the cucumbers with the salt. Set the colander over a bowl and refrigerate for at least 1 hour and up to 2 hours.

4. Using clean hands, squeeze handfuls of cucumber slices to release any excess liquid, and transfer the cucumbers to a medium nonreactive bowl.

5. In another medium nonreactive bowl, combine the white vinegar, cider vinegar, and sugar. Stir until the sugar has completely dissolved. Pour the vinegar mixture over the cucumbers, add the chopped chives, and stir to thoroughly combine. Serve immediately, or refrigerate for up to 12 hours or overnight, and serve cold.

4 to 6 servings

EMERIL'S SLOW-COOKED BAM-B-Q BAKED BEANS

There are all types of baked beans: simmered, sweet, sour, mustardy . . . but just wait until you try these. The secret ingredients here are barbecue sauce and coffee. My mom, Hilda, would be proud.

4 slices bacon, diced

1 large onion, chopped

1½ tablespoons minced garlic

2 sprigs fresh thyme

1 pound dried navy beans, rinsed and picked over

1 cup brewed coffee

½ cup Emeril's Kicked Up Bam B-Q Barbecue Sauce or your favorite barbecue sauce

¼ cup plus 1 tablespoon packed dark brown sugar

1½ tablespoons Creole mustard or other whole-grain brown mustard

1 tablespoon molasses

1 teaspoon red hot sauce

¼ teaspoon freshly ground black pepper

8 cups water

2 teaspoons salt

1. Preheat the oven to 300°F.

2. In a heavy cast-iron Dutch oven, cook the bacon over medium-high heat until the fat has rendered and the bacon is crisp, 4 to 6 minutes. Add the onion and cook, stirring, until it is softened and lightly caramelized, 3 to 4 minutes. Add the garlic and thyme, and cook for 1 minute longer. Then add the beans, coffee, barbecue sauce, brown sugar, mustard, molasses, hot sauce, and pepper, and stir to combine well. Add the water and salt, raise the heat, and bring to a boil. Cover the pot, transfer it to the oven, and bake for 2 hours, undisturbed.

3. Remove the pot from the oven, and stir the beans. Re-cover the pot and continue to bake until the beans are tender, about 1 hour longer.

4. When the beans are tender, remove the cover from the pot and continue baking until the liquid has reduced to a thick, sauce-like consistency and the beans are thick and flavorful, 1 to 1¼ hours. Remove the pot from the oven, and remove the thyme sprigs. Adjust the seasoning if necessary, and serve the beans either hot or warm.

6 servings

CAST-IRON HONEY CORNBREAD

Cornbread is a Southern must, though typically in the South it is salty and contains no sugar . . . but check out this recipe. The cornbread is savory but is lathered with a honey-butter mixture when it comes off the grill. We serve a version of this at my restaurant in Gulfport and folks just go crazy for it. Try using the best local honey available.

2 cups yellow cornmeal

1/2 teaspoon baking powder

1/2 teaspoon baking soda

1 teaspoon sugar

3/4 teaspoon salt

1 1/2 cups buttermilk

1 large egg, lightly beaten

5 tablespoons unsalted butter, melted

1 tablespoon vegetable oil

4 tablespoons (1/2 stick) plus 1 tablespoon unsalted butter, at room temperature

1/4 cup plus 2 tablespoons honey

1. Preheat a grill to low, and place a shallow 12-inch cast-iron skillet or low-rimmed 12-inch cast-iron quesadilla pan on the grill. Let the skillet become hot.

2. While the skillet is heating, combine the cornmeal, baking powder, baking soda, sugar, and salt in a mixing bowl and mix well. In a separate bowl, combine the buttermilk, egg, and melted butter and stir to combine. Add the wet ingredients to the dry ingredients, and stir until just combined.

3. Use the vegetable oil and the 1 tablespoon butter to evenly coat the inside of the preheated skillet. Pour the batter into the skillet, close the lid of the grill, and cook until the cornbread is firm and a toothpick inserted into it comes out clean, 10 to 12 minutes.

4. While the cornbread is cooking, make the honey-butter by combining the remaining 4 tablespoons butter and the honey in a small bowl and stirring until well blended.

5. Remove the skillet from the grill and baste the cornbread with the honey-butter mixture. Let the cornbread sit for 5 minutes before removing it from the skillet. Serve immediately.

One 12-inch cornbread, 6 to 8 servings

BACON POTATO SALAD

How can you go wrong with potatoes and bacon? This salad is deceptively simple and an ideal grilling side.

2 pounds small red potatoes, quartered

3/4 teaspoon salt

1/4 teaspoon cayenne pepper

1/4 teaspoon freshly ground black pepper

2 tablespoons freshly squeezed lemon juice

1/3 cup finely chopped celery

2 tablespoons finely chopped green onions, white and green parts

1 tablespoon chopped fresh parsley

4 hard-boiled eggs, coarsely chopped

3/4 cup mayonnaise

1 1/2 tablespoons Creole or other whole-grain mustard

4 strips crisp-cooked bacon, crumbled

1. Place the potatoes in a saucepan, add water to cover, and bring to a boil. Cook, partially covered, until the potatoes are fork-tender, about 10 minutes.

2. Drain the potatoes and transfer them to a salad bowl. While the potatoes are still warm, season them with the salt, cayenne, black pepper, and lemon juice. Toss well to combine. Add the celery, green onions, parsley, and eggs.

3. In a small bowl, stir the mayonnaise and mustard together. Add this to the salad. Sprinkle the bacon over the salad, and toss gently but thoroughly to mix well.

4. Serve immediately, or refrigerate, covered, and serve slightly chilled.

6 to 8 servings

GRILLED SWEET POTATO SALAD

There is nothing more "Louisiana" than sweet potatoes. We eat them baked, boiled, smashed, grilled, in gravies and casseroles—you name it. Well, here's our tribute to this incredible ingredient.

2 pounds sweet potatoes, peeled and cut into ½-inch-thick rounds

¼ cup plus 3 tablespoons olive oil

1 teaspoon salt

½ teaspoon freshly ground black pepper

1½ tablespoons freshly squeezed lime juice, or more to taste

1½ tablespoons roughly chopped fresh cilantro

¼ cup very thinly shaved red onion

1½ tablespoons crumbled Cotija cheese (or other mild crumbly cheese, such as farmer's cheese)

1. Preheat a grill to medium-high and the oven to 350°F.

2. Place the sweet potatoes in a bowl, and add the 3 tablespoons olive oil, salt, and pepper. Toss well. Then place the potatoes on the grill and cook until nice grill marks develop, 2 to 3 minutes on each side.

3. Transfer the potatoes to a baking sheet, place it in the oven, and bake until they are tender enough to easily pierce with a fork, 20 to 25 minutes. Remove from the oven and set aside to cool to room temperature.

4. Arrange the sweet potato slices on a platter, and drizzle the remaining ¼ cup olive oil and the lime juice over them. Sprinkle with the cilantro, red onion, and cheese, and serve.

4 to 6 servings

BLACK-EYED PEA SALAD

Black-eyed peas aren't just for New Year's. I love them in salads, cooked in their own broth, inside fritters . . . as anything, with anything. Here they are, in all their glory.

5 cups cooked and drained black-eyed peas

4 slices bacon, cooked until crisp and crumbled, fat reserved separately

1/2 cup plus 2 tablespoons red wine vinegar

1/2 cup olive oil

1/2 cup finely chopped red onion

1/2 cup finely chopped red bell pepper

3 tablespoons finely chopped green onions, white and green parts

2 tablespoons finely chopped jalapeños

2 tablespoons finely chopped fresh parsley

1 1/2 teaspoons minced garlic

1 1/2 teaspoons Emeril's Original Essence or Creole Seasoning (page 25)

3/4 teaspoon salt, plus more if needed

1/2 teaspoon freshly ground black pepper, plus more if needed

1. Combine the black-eyed peas, crumbled bacon, 3 tablespoons of the reserved bacon fat, and all the remaining ingredients in a large bowl, and toss well to combine. Cover and refrigerate for at least 4 hours, or preferably overnight, stirring occasionally.

2. Remove the salad from the refrigerator 30 minutes before serving, and allow it to come to room temperature. Toss it well just before serving; taste, and re-season if necessary.

8 servings

WARM-WEATHER POTATO SALAD

A simple vinaigrette stands in for the usual mayo here. Delicious!

2 pounds small red potatoes, quartered

1 small (5-ounce) white onion, halved

3 tablespoons white balsamic vinegar

1 tablespoon cider vinegar

1/2 teaspoon Dijon mustard

1/4 teaspoon honey

1/4 cup olive oil

1 tablespoon minced shallots

1 tablespoon chopped fresh chervil

2 teaspoons chopped fresh chives

1 teaspoon chopped fresh parsley

1 teaspoon chopped fresh cilantro

1 teaspoon salt

1/2 teaspoon freshly ground white pepper

1. Place the potatoes and the onion in a pot and add enough salted water to cover by at least 3 inches. Bring the water to a boil and immediately reduce to a simmer. Cook until the potatoes are tender, about 15 minutes.

2. Meanwhile, make the dressing by combining the white balsamic vinegar, cider vinegar, Dijon mustard, and honey in a small mixing bowl. Whisk to combine. Slowly drizzle in the olive oil in a slow, steady stream, stirring constantly. Stir in the shallots, chervil, chives, parsley, cilantro, 1/2 teaspoon of the salt, and 1/4 teaspoon of the pepper. Let the dressing sit for at least 10 minutes at room temperature for the herbs to infuse their flavor.

3. Drain the potatoes and discard the onion. Transfer the potatoes to a serving bowl. Stir the dressing just before pouring it over the potatoes, season with the remaining salt and pepper, and toss to coat well. Serve warm or at room temperature.

4 servings

GRILLED CORN WITH CHEESE AND CHILI

This dish owes its inspiration to our Louisiana neighbors on two sides: the incredible sweet corn that is grown in Indianola, Mississippi, where some of my wife's family is from, and also the wonderful Tex-Mex flavors of our friends in Texas.

6 ears fresh sweet corn, silk removed but husks still attached

1/2 cup sour cream

2 tablespoons whole milk

3 tablespoons butter, melted

1 lime, halved

1/2 cup finely grated queso añejo, queso fresco, or Parmesan cheese

1 tablespoon chili powder

1 1/2 teaspoons kosher salt

1. Pull the husks up to cover the ears of corn, and place the corn in a large bowl or pot. Cover with cold water, and place a large plate or other weight on top of the corn so that it remains submerged. Allow the corn to soak for at least 1 hour or as long as 4 hours.

2. Meanwhile, combine the sour cream and milk in a small bowl, and set it aside.

3. Preheat a grill to medium-high. Adjust the grilling rack so that it sits about 4 inches away from the fire.

4. Drain the corn but do not remove the husks. Lay the corn on the grill and cook, turning it frequently, until it is crisp-tender, 15 to 20 minutes. Remove the corn from the grill and allow it to cool slightly. Then pull the husks back to form a handle, and brush the ears evenly with the melted butter. Squeeze the lime halves evenly over the ears of corn. Return the corn to the grill and cook, turning it occasionally, for 5 to 10 minutes, or until the corn is slightly browned in places. Remove the corn from the heat and brush the ears with some of the sour cream mixture. Divide the cheese evenly among the ears of corn, coating them on all sides. Sprinkle with the chili powder and kosher salt, and serve immediately.

6 servings

GRILLED ASPARAGUS WITH GARLIC

If you have a grill basket, I highly recommend using it for cooking asparagus on the grill. If not, make sure to position the asparagus so that they lie perpendicular to the grill grates, so they don't fall through. This dish can also be done indoors in a grill pan, if you'd like.

1 pound large asparagus, woody ends trimmed

3 tablespoons extra-virgin olive oil

3/4 teaspoon kosher salt

1/4 teaspoon freshly ground black pepper

1/2 teaspoon freshly squeezed lemon juice

2 teaspoons minced garlic

1. Preheat a grill to medium.

2. In a shallow baking dish, toss the asparagus with the oil to coat well. Add the salt and pepper, and toss to coat evenly.

3. Place the asparagus on the grill in a single layer, and cook, turning occasionally, until the spears are marked and tender, 12 to 15 minutes. Transfer the asparagus to a platter, sprinkle with the lemon juice and garlic, and toss to combine. Cover with aluminum foil and let sit for 5 minutes before serving.

4 servings

WATERCRESS, AVOCADO, AND MANGO SALAD

I love this salad with the Soft-Shell Crabs on the Grill on page 114. What a dynamite combination!

½ cup freshly squeezed pink grapefruit juice

1 tablespoon honey

1 teaspoon minced shallot

½ teaspoon Dijon mustard

¼ teaspoon minced garlic

½ cup extra-virgin olive oil

1 tablespoon chopped fresh basil

Salt and freshly ground black pepper to taste

6 ounces fresh watercress sprigs

1 cup diced fresh mango

1 Hass avocado, peeled, pitted, and cut into 6 wedges

1. Place the grapefruit juice in a small nonreactive saucepan and simmer until it is reduced to 1/4 cup, 3 to 4 minutes. Set it aside to cool.

2. In a medium bowl, combine the cooled reduced grapefruit juice, honey, shallot, mustard, and garlic and whisk to blend. While continuing to whisk, add the oil in a slow, steady drizzle until it is fully incorporated. Stir in the basil, and season with salt and pepper to taste.

3. In a large salad bowl, combine the watercress, mango, and 1/4 cup of the vinaigrette. Season lightly with salt and pepper, and toss to combine. Arrange the avocado on top, and drizzle with more vinaigrette if desired.

6 servings

GRILLED GARLIC BREAD

My kids absolutely adore this simple, delicious garlic bread. Goes with anything . . . you name it.

8 tablespoons (1 stick) unsalted butter, at room temperature

1 tablespoon minced fresh parsley

2 teaspoons minced garlic

1 teaspoon Emeril's Original Essence or Creole Seasoning (page 25)

1 teaspoon freshly squeezed lemon juice

1/8 teaspoon salt

1 loaf French or Italian bread, about 22 inches long

1. Preheat a grill to medium-high.

2. In a bowl, cream the butter, parsley, garlic, Original Essence, lemon juice, and salt together until well blended.

3. Slice the loaf of bread in half horizontally. Brush the cut side of each piece evenly with the garlic-butter mixture, and place the halves back together. Wrap tightly in aluminum foil. Place the foil package on the grill and cook, turning occasionally, until the bread is crisp on the outside and warmed through, 10 to 12 minutes.

4. Remove the bread from the grill and keep it warm in the oven, still in the foil, until ready to serve. Slice the bread crosswise into serving pieces, and serve hot.

6 servings

BABY SPINACH–JICAMA SALAD

Many folks aren't familiar with this light brown root vegetable. It has a white center with a flavor somewhere between mild celery and pear. I find that its crunchy texture is delightful in salads. If you can't find jicama at your supermarket, try a market that features Latino produce.

3 tablespoons freshly squeezed
    orange juice

1 tablespoon champagne vinegar

1 teaspoon minced shallot

1 teaspoon honey

1/2 teaspoon Dijon mustard

1/2 teaspoon minced garlic

1/2 teaspoon grated orange zest

1/2 cup olive oil

1/4 teaspoon salt, plus more to taste

1/8 teaspoon freshly ground
    black pepper, plus more
    to taste

4 teaspoons chopped fresh cilantro

6 ounces baby spinach,
    rinsed and spun dry

1 cup peeled, julienned jicama

1/2 cup diced ripe tomatoes

1. In a small mixing bowl, combine the orange juice, vinegar, shallot, honey, mustard, garlic, and orange zest. Whisk to combine. While whisking, add the olive oil in a slow, steady stream until fully incorporated. Add the 1/4 teaspoon salt and the 1/8 teaspoon black pepper, and stir in the chopped cilantro.

2. In a medium bowl, combine the baby spinach, jicama, and tomatoes. Add 1/4 cup of the vinaigrette, toss, and season the salad with salt and pepper to taste.

4 servings

GRILLED MIXED MUSHROOMS ON SKEWERS WITH FRESH HERBS AND PARMESAN

I love mushrooms, but when you throw garlic, herbs, and Parmesan cheese into the mix, how can you miss? Try these simple skewers alongside a juicy grilled steak.

Six 12-inch bamboo skewers, soaked in warm water for at least 15 minutes

6 ounces shiitake mushrooms, stemmed

6 ounces cremini mushrooms, stemmed

6 ounces baby bello mushrooms, stemmed

6 ounces button mushrooms, stemmed

2 tablespoons chopped garlic

1 teaspoon kosher salt, plus more to taste

1/2 teaspoon freshly ground black pepper, plus more to taste

1/4 cup white balsamic vinegar

1/2 cup extra-virgin olive oil

1/2 cup finely grated Parmigiano-Reggiano cheese

1/4 cup chopped fresh parsley

2 tablespoons chopped fresh thyme

2 tablespoons chopped fresh rosemary

1/2 cup olive oil

1. Preheat a grill to medium-high.

2. Halve any mushrooms that are large. Evenly divide the mix of mushrooms among the skewers. Arrange the skewers on a baking sheet or large platter.

3. In a small bowl, combine the garlic, salt, pepper, and vinegar. Whisk in the extra-virgin olive oil in a slow, steady stream. Add the Parmesan and the fresh herbs.

4. Drizzle the olive oil over the skewered mushrooms and rotate the skewers in the oil to coat all sides.

5. Grill the mushrooms, turning the skewers every minute, until they are nicely browned, about 4 minutes. Brush some of the herb-Parmesan mixture over the mushrooms and grill for 1 minute longer. Remove the skewers from the grill and season the mushrooms with salt and pepper.

6. To serve, arrange the skewers on a platter and drizzle them with more of the remaining herb-Parmesan mixture. (Any unused herb-Parmesan mixture can be saved in an airtight nonreactive container in the refrigerator and used as an accompaniment to pasta, bread, or grilled fish or chicken.)

6 servings

EGGPLANT AND PEPPERS WITH FETA

There is something about eggplant that I really love, and when you grill it, an amazing thing happens to the taste and texture that is truly delicious. Grilling adds a smoky flavor that I cannot resist.

2 large eggplants, ends trimmed, sliced into 1/3-inch-thick rounds

Salt

1 red bell pepper, cored, seeded, and sliced lengthwise into 8 pieces

1 yellow bell pepper, cored, seeded, and sliced lengthwise into 8 pieces

1 green bell pepper, cored, seeded, and sliced lengthwise into 8 pieces

1 orange bell pepper, cored, seeded, and sliced lengthwise into 8 pieces

1/3 cup olive oil

Kosher salt and freshly ground black pepper

1/3 cup feta cheese, crumbled (3 ounces)

1 tablespoon minced fresh marjoram, oregano, or basil, or a combination

1/4 cup extra-virgin olive oil

Juice of 1 lemon

1. Place the eggplant slices on a wire rack and sprinkle them lightly with salt on both sides. Set the rack aside until the eggplant begins to "sweat," usually 15 to 20 minutes. Blot the eggplant dry with clean paper towels.

2. Preheat a grill to medium-high.

3. Arrange the eggplant and all the bell pepper slices on a large baking sheet, and brush both sides of all the pieces with the olive oil. Season with kosher salt and black pepper. Transfer the eggplant and peppers to the grill, in batches if necessary, and cook, turning them occasionally to promote even browning, until they are softened and nicely marked, 15 to 20 minutes.

4. Transfer the grilled eggplant slices to a large platter, and top them with the pepper strips. Garnish with the crumbled feta and minced marjoram. Drizzle with the olive oil and lemon juice, and serve either warm or at room temperature.

8 to 10 servings

GRILLED POLENTA

The great thing about this dish is that the polenta can be prepared up to two days ahead of time, set to cool in the fridge, and then brought out just before you're ready to grill for a quick and easy side. Don't be afraid to coat the grill grates and the polenta liberally with olive oil, and take care to use very clean grill grates—those are the secrets to keeping the polenta from sticking to the grill. Serve with drizzled olive oil and Parmesan cheese. Spectacular!

2½ cups whole milk

2½ cups water

2 teaspoons kosher salt

½ teaspoon freshly ground white pepper

2 cups yellow cornmeal

3 tablespoons unsalted butter

½ cup (4 ounces) mascarpone cheese

2 tablespoons unsalted butter, at room temperature

½ cup olive oil

1. In a 2½-quart or larger saucepan, bring the milk, water, salt, and pepper to a low boil, being careful not to allow the liquid to boil over. Working quickly, vigorously whisk in the cornmeal (to avoid lumps). Reduce the heat to low and cook for 20 minutes, stirring frequently with a heat-resistant rubber spatula. (Make sure to stir along the sides and bottom of the pan so the polenta does not stick.) Once the polenta is tender, remove the pan from the heat and stir in the 3 tablespoons butter and the mascarpone cheese.

2. Cut two pieces of parchment paper to line a 13 X 9-inch rimmed baking sheet. Lay one piece of parchment on the sheet and brush 1 tablespoon of the room-temperature butter over it. Pour the polenta onto the buttered parchment and spread the polenta into a smooth, even layer. Brush the other piece of parchment with the remaining 1 tablespoon butter and place the parchment, butter side down, on top of the polenta. Refrigerate until firm, at least 2 hours or up to 2 days in advance.

3. Preheat a grill to medium-high.

4. Trim the polenta, cutting off about 1 inch on each side to form straight edges, and cut it into 6 squares.

Halve each square to form 2 triangles. You should have 12 triangular pieces.

5. Make sure the grill is well cleaned, and oil it with some of the olive oil. Brush the top of the polenta squares generously with olive oil, and place the polenta, oiled side down, on the grill. Brush the tops with olive oil. After about 3 minutes, rotate the polenta 90 degrees to make grill crosshatch marks. (If you try to turn or move the polenta before a crust has formed on the grill side, it will stick.) Cook for an additional 3 minutes. Turn the polenta squares over and repeat, cooking until they are nicely browned and crisp, about 6 minutes longer. Serve hot.

8 to 12 servings

GRILLED CAPONATA

Smoky grilled eggplant, peppers, and onions combine here to make something truly out of this world. If you're a caponata-lover like me, this will blow your mind. Make a big batch of this and make a few new friends. This is delicious on its own, spooned over simply grilled fish or chicken, tossed with pasta, or served with slices of hearty bread for dipping.

2 large globe eggplants (about 2 pounds), ends trimmed, sliced into 3/4-inch-thick rounds

Salt

3 large red bell peppers (about 1 1/2 pounds)

3/4 cup olive oil

2 medium onions, sliced into 3/4-inch-thick rounds

1 pound cherry or grape tomatoes (about 1 pint), halved

3/4 cup diced celery (small dice)

1 tablespoon minced garlic

1/4 cup red wine vinegar

1 teaspoon sugar

1/2 teaspoon crushed red pepper

1/2 cup chopped pitted Kalamata olives

1/4 cup drained nonpareil capers

1/2 cup finely slivered fresh basil

3/4 cup extra-virgin olive oil

Kosher salt and freshly ground black pepper

1. Preheat a grill to medium-high.

2. Place the eggplant slices on a wire rack and sprinkle them lightly with salt on both sides. Set the rack aside until the eggplant begins to "sweat," usually 15 to 20 minutes.

3. Meanwhile, coat the bell peppers with some of the olive oil and grill them, turning them periodically, until their skin is blistered and blackened, 10 minutes. Remove the peppers from the grill, place them in a bowl, and cover it tightly with plastic wrap. Set the bowl aside.

4. Coat the onions with some of the olive oil and grill them for 3 minutes on each side. Transfer them to a platter.

5. Lightly dry the eggplant slices with paper towels, and brush each side generously with the remaining olive oil. Grill the eggplant for 4 minutes on each side, and add it to the platter with the onions.

6. Place the tomatoes in a large bowl. Add the celery, garlic, vinegar, sugar, and crushed red pepper. Mix to combine.

7. Cut the grilled onions and eggplant into ¾-inch dice and add them to the bowl. Peel and seed the grilled bell peppers, cut them into ¾-inch pieces, and add them to the bowl.

8. Add the olives, capers, basil, and extra-virgin olive oil. Stir well to combine. Season the caponata with kosher salt and black pepper to taste. Serve warm or at room temperature.

About 8 servings

GRILLED FENNEL, GREEN BEAN, AND GREEN ONION SALAD WITH FRESH HERBS

Talk about a great combo! I've always felt that fennel really comes to life when you grill it, and with the grilled green beans added, it's truly a hit. Light and refreshing.

¼ cup sliced chives, cut about 1 inch long on the diagonal

2 tablespoons diced shallots (small dice)

2 tablespoons chopped fresh parsley

2 teaspoons grated orange zest

1 teaspoon sugar

½ teaspoon freshly ground black pepper

½ cup freshly squeezed orange juice

¼ cup extra-virgin olive oil

2 pounds fennel (about 3 bulbs), tops removed

½ cup olive oil

8 ounces green beans, ends trimmed

4 ounces green onions (about 2 bunches), root ends trimmed

Kosher salt

1. Preheat a grill to medium-high.

2. Combine the chives, shallots, parsley, orange zest, sugar, pepper, and orange juice in a large bowl. Whisk in the extra-virgin olive oil.

3. Cut each fennel bulb into 1-inch wedges, leaving the core intact. Trim off any brown edges and any excess core (you need just enough core to hold the fennel pieces together). Place the fennel in a bowl, add the olive oil, and toss. Lay the fennel on a tray.

4. Toss the green beans, and then the green onions, in the olive oil and lay them on the tray with the fennel. Sprinkle the vegetables with kosher salt.

5. Grill the fennel until tender, about 4 minutes on each side. Grill the green beans until just crisp-tender, 8 to 10 minutes (don't turn them—flipped beans may fall through the grates). Grill the green onions until wilted, about 1 minute on each side.

6. Add the grilled vegetables to the bowl with the herb mixture. Toss well, adjust the seasoning if necessary, and serve warm or at room temperature.

6 servings

GRILLED CAULIFLOWER WITH ROASTED SHALLOT–GARLIC BUTTER

Try grilled cauliflower—I guarantee that you will want it again and again. The caramelized edges bring out a sweet, nutty flavor, and the shallot butter that it's tossed in at the end . . . oh, baby, don't make me talk about it.

4 large shallots, halved lengthwise

3 tablespoons olive oil

Kosher salt and freshly ground black pepper

4 tablespoons (1/2 stick) unsalted butter, at room temperature

1 teaspoon minced garlic

1/2 teaspoon freshly squeezed lemon juice

1 large cauliflower, cut into large florets

1. Preheat the oven to 450°F. Line a small baking dish with aluminum foil.

2. Place the shallots in the prepared baking dish and drizzle them with 1 tablespoon of the olive oil. Season with kosher salt and pepper. Roast until they are soft and caramelized, turning them if necessary to promote even browning, 15 to 20 minutes. Set the shallots aside to cool.

3. When they have cooled, finely chop the roasted shallots and transfer them to a small bowl. Add the butter, garlic, lemon juice, 1/4 teaspoon kosher salt, and 1/8 teaspoon pepper, and mix well to combine. Set the shallot-garlic butter aside while you grill the cauliflower.

4. Preheat a grill to medium.

5. Brush the cauliflower with the remaining 2 tablespoons olive oil and place the florets on the grill. Cover the grill, reduce the heat to medium-low, and cook until the florets are golden on the bottom edges, 4 to 5 minutes. Continue cooking, turning them frequently, until they are evenly browned around the edges and crisp-tender, 5 to 7 minutes longer. Transfer the cauliflower to a large bowl, and add the shallot-garlic butter. Toss to combine. Season to taste with kosher salt and pepper, and serve either hot or warm.

4 servings

TOMATOES ON THE FENCE

What a great way to use the sweet cherry tomatoes of summer! Explore your local farmers' markets to get small tomatoes of all shapes and colors . . . and don't forget the simple basil-garlic oil for a huge hit.

. . . .

24 to 30 large cherry, cherub, or grape tomatoes, preferably in different colors

Six 4- to 6-inch bamboo skewers, soaked in warm water for 1 hour

1/2 cup extra-virgin olive oil

3/4 teaspoon sea salt, plus more if needed

1/2 teaspoon freshly ground black pepper, plus more if needed

1/2 cup coarsely chopped fresh basil

1 tablespoon minced garlic

1. Preheat a grill to medium-high.

2. Skewer 4 or 5 tomatoes onto each skewer and brush them lightly with some of the olive oil. Sprinkle the tomatoes with ½ teaspoon of the sea salt and ¼ teaspoon of the pepper. Grill them briefly, turning them occasionally, until they are just warmed through and barely marked by the grill, 2 to 3 minutes. Transfer the tomato skewers to a serving platter.

3. In a small mixing bowl, combine the remaining olive oil with the basil and garlic. Season with the remaining ¼ teaspoon salt and ¼ teaspoon pepper, and stir to blend. Spoon the mixture evenly over the tomatoes, and sprinkle with additional sea salt and pepper if desired. Serve warm or at room temperature.

4 to 6 servings

Sandwiches, WRAPS, and PIZZAS

GRILLED FIG AND GOAT CHEESE PIZZAS

This is a dynamite starter to any meal when figs are in season. The great thing is that this crust can be used with any topping combination you dream up! Make sure you generously sprinkle the pizza peel with cornmeal to help the pizza slide off easily onto the grill.

. . . .

One ¼-ounce packet active
  dry yeast

¾ cup warm water (about 110°F)

2 cups all-purpose flour,
  plus more for dusting

½ teaspoon salt

2 tablespoons plus 1½ teaspoons
  vegetable oil, plus more for
  the grill

1 tablespoon heavy cream

8 ounces goat cheese,
  at room temperature

5 tablespoons honey

Cornmeal, for sprinkling on the
  pizza peel

1 pound ripe fresh figs, rinsed
  and patted dry, stems removed,
  sliced ¼ inch thick

⅛ teaspoon freshly ground
  black pepper

8 fresh mint leaves,
  torn into pieces

1 tablespoon Armagnac or brandy

1. To make the dough, combine the yeast, water, and 1 tablespoon of the flour in a medium bowl, and whisk to blend. Let the mixture stand until it is slightly foamy, about 5 minutes.

2. Combine the remaining flour and the salt in a large bowl, and stir to blend. Add the yeast mixture, the 2 tablespoons oil, and the cream. Stir well with a heavy wooden spoon until the dough begins to come together and pull away from the sides of the bowl. Turn it out onto a lightly floured surface and knead for 4 to 5 minutes into a smooth, but slightly sticky, dough. Oil a clean bowl with 1 teaspoon of the remaining vegetable oil and place the dough in the bowl, turning to coat it. Cover the bowl with plastic wrap or a clean kitchen towel, and allow the dough to rise in a warm, draft-free place until doubled in size, about 40 minutes.

3. Lightly grease a baking sheet with the remaining ½ teaspoon vegetable oil. Divide the dough in half, and form each piece into a ball. Place them on the prepared baking sheet, cover with plastic wrap, and refrigerate until doubled in volume, about 2 hours.

4. Preheat a grill to medium. Clean the grill very well with a brush, and lightly grease the grate with vegetable oil.

5. Combine the goat cheese and 3 tablespoons of the honey in a bowl, and mash with a fork until smooth.

6. Remove the dough from the refrigerator and roll each ball with a rolling pin on a floured surface into a 10-inch round. Transfer one of the rounds to a pizza peel sprinkled with cornmeal. With a quick flick of the wrist, slide the pizza dough onto the grill and cook on one side, rotating it with a spatula to mark it evenly, until golden brown, 3 to 4 minutes. Remove the dough from the grill and place it, grilled side up, on a large cutting board. Repeat with the remaining dough.

7. Spread half of the goat cheese mixture across each crust, using a rubber spatula. Arrange half of the sliced figs across the top of each crust.

8. Transfer the pizzas to the grill, cover, and cook until golden brown, rotating them with a spatula to keep them from burning, 3 to 4 minutes. Transfer the pizzas to serving plates, and sprinkle them with the black pepper and the mint leaves. In a small bowl, combine the remaining 2 tablespoons honey with the Armagnac. Drizzle each pizza with half of the honey-Armagnac mixture, and serve immediately.

Two 10-inch pizzas, 6 to 8 servings

Oven-Baked Fig and Goat Cheese Pizzas

1. Place a pizza stone if you have one in the oven and preheat the oven to 500°F.

2. Remove the dough from the refrigerator and roll each ball out into a 10-inch round on a lightly floured pizza peel or large chopping board. Make "dimples" with your fingertips in the top of the dough. Spread half of the goat cheese mixture across each round, using a rubber spatula. Spread half of the sliced figs across the top of each round.

3. Transfer the rounds to the pizza stone (or to two heavy baking sheets) and bake until golden brown, about 12 minutes. Remove them from the oven, transfer them to serving plates, and finish as described.

GRILLED GREEN ONION FLATBREAD

This easy, delicious flatbread grills up nicely, and folks love snacking on its crisp, green-oniony goodness. Whip up a batch to accompany a salad or a spread, or serve it with just about any grilling menu.

1 teaspoon active dry yeast

1/2 teaspoon sugar

1/2 cup warm water (about 110°F)

1 1/4 cups all-purpose flour, plus more as needed

1/2 teaspoon salt

2 tablespoons minced green onions, white and green parts

2 tablespoons butter, melted and kept warm

4 tablespoons extra-virgin olive oil

Emeril's Original Essence or Creole Seasoning (page 25)

1. In a glass measuring cup, combine the yeast and the sugar. Add the water and stir well. Set aside until foamy, about 5 minutes.

2. Sift the flour and salt together into a large bowl. Add the green onions and toss to coat. Make a well in the center of the flour and pour the yeast mixture, warm butter, and 2 tablespoons of the olive oil into the well. Mix together with your fingers until a smooth, just slightly sticky dough forms, working in a small amount of additional flour if needed.

3. Transfer the dough to a lightly floured surface and knead it for 3 minutes.

4. Oil a small bowl with 1 teaspoon of the remaining olive oil, and place the dough in the bowl, turning to coat it. Cover the bowl with plastic wrap or a damp kitchen towel, and let it rest in a warm, draft-free place until the dough has doubled in size, about 1 hour.

5. Preheat a grill to high and lightly grease the grill grate.

6. Divide the dough into 6 equal pieces, and transfer them to a lightly floured work surface. Using a lightly floured rolling pin, gently roll each portion of dough into a round that is 5 or 6 inches in diameter.

7. Transfer the rounds of dough to the prepared grill and cook until slightly puffed, lightly golden, and marked on both sides, about 3 minutes per side.

8. Place the flatbreads on a platter and drizzle them with the remaining olive oil. Sprinkle lightly with Original Essence to taste, and serve immediately.

Six 5- to 6-inch flatbreads

FAJITA PANINI WITH CHIPOTLE MAYONNAISE

Oh yeah, babe. Don't skip the Chipotle Mayonnaise here—it'll knock your socks off!

1 pound top round or sirloin, sliced into 1/4-inch-wide strips

2 cloves garlic, peeled and smashed

1 teaspoon kosher salt

1/4 teaspoon freshly ground black pepper

1/4 cup freshly squeezed lemon juice

1/2 teaspoon ground cumin

2 tablespoons plus 8 teaspoons vegetable oil

1 medium onion, halved and thinly sliced

1/2 green bell pepper, stemmed, seeded, and sliced into 1/4-inch-wide strips

1/2 red bell pepper, stemmed, seeded, and sliced into 1/4-inch-wide strips

1/2 yellow bell pepper, stemmed, seeded, and sliced into 1/4-inch-wide strips

1/2 teaspoon minced garlic

1/4 teaspoon salt

Pinch of freshly ground black pepper

Chipotle Mayonnaise (recipe follows)

8 thin slices ciabatta or other rustic Italian white bread

4 ounces Pepper Jack cheese, shredded

Your favorite salsa, for garnish (optional)

Fresh cilantro sprigs, for garnish (optional)

1. Place the top round or sirloin strips, smashed garlic, kosher salt, pepper, lemon juice, and cumin in a resealable plastic bag and marinate at room temperature for 30 minutes.

2. Remove the steak from the marinade. (Discard the marinade.) Heat the 2 tablespoons vegetable oil in a large skillet over medium-high heat. Add the onions and cook, stirring, for 2 minutes. Add the steak and the bell peppers and cook, stirring, for 2 minutes. Add the minced garlic and cook an additional 1 to 2 minutes, or until the steak is at the desired degree of doneness. Season with the salt and pepper, remove from the heat, and set aside.

3. Spread 1 tablespoon of the Chipotle Mayonnaise over each slice of bread. Divide the steak mixture over 4 pieces of bread. Top with the shredded cheese and the remaining bread, mayonnaise side down.

4. Heat a grill pan over high heat. Spread 1 teaspoon of the vegetable oil over the top and 1 teaspoon over the bottom of each panini. Place the paninis on the hot grill pan and place a skillet or panini press on top. Cook for 1 to 2 minutes. Turn the paninis over, and cook until the cheese is melted and the sandwiches are golden brown on both sides, about 2 minutes longer.

5. Serve hot, with salsa and cilantro sprigs if desired.

4 servings

Chipotle Mayonnaise

1/2 cup plus 2 tablespoons mayonnaise
1 chipotle chile in adobo sauce, seeds removed, roughly chopped (about 2 teaspoons)
2 teaspoons adobo sauce
1/2 teaspoon minced garlic
1/4 teaspoon salt
1/8 teaspoon crushed dried oregano

Place all the ingredients in a blender or food processor and blend on high speed until smooth, about 30 seconds. Transfer to a clean container and refrigerate until ready to use. This will keep up to 2 weeks. **About 3/4 cup**

VIETNAMESE-STYLE GRILLED PORK PO'BOY

I have such love for the Vietnamese people who have enriched our New Orleans community in countless ways since their arrival in the 1970s. This dish is my version of their po'boy, also known as *bahn mi*. If you want to kick things up even further, try using some of the Kicked-Up Vietnamese-Style Mayonnaise on page 79 instead of the plain mayonnaise.

2 green onions, minced, white and light green parts

1 fresh red or green chile, such as Thai, jalapeño, or serrano, seeded and minced

2 cloves garlic, minced

1 tablespoon sugar

1/4 teaspoon freshly ground black pepper

2 tablespoons Vietnamese fish sauce (nuoc nam)

1 1/2 tablespoons freshly squeezed lime juice

1 pork tenderloin (about 1 1/2 pounds), trimmed

2 teaspoons vegetable oil

1 baguette, about 24 inches long

Mayonnaise, to taste

1/2 seedless cucumber, peeled and thinly sliced

Pickled Carrots and Daikon (recipe follows)

3 jalapeño or serrano chiles, seeded and thinly sliced

Fresh cilantro leaves, to taste

1. In a resealable plastic bag, combine the green onions, minced chile pepper, garlic, sugar, black pepper, fish sauce, and lime juice, and stir until the sugar has dissolved. Add the pork, turn to coat it evenly, and seal the bag. Allow the pork to marinate, refrigerated, for at least 6 hours and up to overnight, turning it occasionally.

2. Remove the pork from the marinade and set it aside at room temperature for 20 minutes.

3. Meanwhile, preheat a grill to medium-high.

4. Pat the pork dry, and brush it all over with the vegetable oil. Grill the pork, turning it often, until an instant-read thermometer inserted into the center reads 145° to 150°F, 18 to 20 minutes. Remove the pork from the heat and let it rest for 15 minutes. Then cut it into 1/4-inch-thick diagonal slices.

5. Cut the baguette into 4 pieces, each about 6 inches long. Cut each piece in half horizontally. If the bread is very dense, remove some of the interior to hollow the bread slightly. Toast the bread halves lightly, if desired. Spread both sides of the bread liberally (or to taste) with mayonnaise. Divide the sliced pork evenly among the bottom halves of the sandwiches. Top with

the cucumber slices, the Pickled Carrots and Daikon, and the sliced chile peppers. Garnish with the cilantro leaves, and place the tops, mayonnaise side down, on the sandwiches. Cut each sandwich in half, and serve immediately.

4 servings

Pickled Carrots and Daikon

These quick pickled vegetables really make the Vietnamese-style po'boy something special—and they are also a great snack on their own!

1 cup rice vinegar
3 tablespoons sugar
$1/4$ teaspoon crushed red pepper
$1/4$ teaspoon salt
2 carrots, thinly sliced on the diagonal
1 cup thinly sliced daikon

In a small nonreactive saucepan, combine the vinegar, sugar, crushed red pepper, and salt and bring to a boil, stirring until the sugar and salt have dissolved. Remove from the heat and allow to cool slightly. Then transfer the mixture to a nonreactive mixing bowl, and add the carrots and daikon. Stir to combine. Refrigerate, covered, for at least 30 minutes and up to overnight. **About 2 cups**

GRILLED FISH TACOS WITH A ROASTED CHILE AND AVOCADO SALSA

This is such an easy, healthful dish. Use any mild, flaky fish that you like—mahimahi, cod, lemon fish (cobia), amberjack . . . the list goes on. Don't skip the salsa!

1/2 Hass avocado, peeled, pit removed

2 poblano chiles, roasted, peeled, and seeded

1 jalapeño, roasted, peeled, and seeded

1/4 cup plus 2 tablespoons olive oil

3/4 cup chopped onion

3/4 cup cilantro leaves

Juice of 1 lime

1 1/4 teaspoons kosher salt

3 tablespoons water

1 pound amberjack fillet

1/2 teaspoon freshly ground white pepper

8 fresh white or yellow corn tortillas, warmed according to package directions or grilled briefly to heat through

4 slices ripe tomato, cut in half

2 limes, halved

1. In a blender, combine the avocado half with the roasted poblano and jalapeño chiles, the 1/4 cup olive oil, 1/4 cup of the chopped onion, 1/4 cup of the cilantro leaves, the lime juice, 1/4 teaspoon of the kosher salt, and the water. Puree until smooth, and set aside.

2. Preheat a grill to medium, or preheat a cast-iron grill pan over medium heat.

3. Season the amberjack with the remaining 1 teaspoon kosher salt and the white pepper. Rub the remaining 2 tablespoons olive oil over both sides of the fish, and place the fish on the grill. Grill until the fish is just cooked through and flakes easily, about 4 minutes on each side. Remove the fish from the grill, and use a fork to break it into flakes or small chunks.

4. To assemble the tacos, divide the fish evenly among the tortillas. Place 1 tablespoon of the remaining chopped onion and 1 tablespoon of the remaining cilantro leaves over each portion of fish. Place a half tomato slice over each, and drizzle with some of the avocado salsa. Squeeze some lime juice over the tacos, fold the tortilla sides together, and serve immediately.

8 tacos, 4 servings

ROAST TURKEY PANINI WITH PESTO, ROASTED RED PEPPERS, AND FONTINA

This is a great sandwich for leftover turkey if you happen to have some hanging around, but store-bought sliced roast turkey works just as well. Don't skimp on the fontina cheese, 'cause that's what brings it all together. Wow!

8 thin slices ciabatta or other rustic Italian white bread

¼ cup prepared basil pesto

8 ounces very thinly sliced roast turkey breast

1 red bell pepper, roasted, stemmed, skin and seeds removed, cut into thin strips

6 ounces fontina cheese, thinly sliced

1 tablespoon extra-virgin olive oil

1. Arrange the slices of bread on a flat work surface, and using a small spoon, divide the pesto evenly among them. Spread the pesto over the bread.

2. Divide the turkey, roasted pepper strips, and fontina equally among 4 bread slices. Top with the remaining 4 slices of bread, pesto side down, to form 4 sandwiches.

3. Brush the outside of each sandwich lightly with some of the olive oil.

4. Preheat a grill to medium-high or heat a large grill pan over medium-high heat.

5. Place the sandwiches on the grill and cook, pressing them occasionally with a large metal spatula or the bottom of a small heavy saucepan, until the bread is golden brown and the cheese has melted, about 4 minutes per side. Transfer the sandwiches to a cutting board, slice them in half on the diagonal, and serve immediately.

4 servings

GRILLED PIZZAS WITH PROSCIUTTO, PESTO, AND TALEGGIO CHEESE

This grilled pizza brings back some of my fondest food memories from trips to Italy. I just love the combination of salty prosciutto and creamy Taleggio.

2 tablespoons olive oil

¼ cup all-purpose flour

Basic Pizza Dough
   (recipe follows)

Cornmeal, for sprinkling on the
   pizza peel

¼ cup prepared basil pesto

4 ounces thinly sliced prosciutto

⅔ cup grated Taleggio cheese

1. Preheat a grill to medium, and lightly oil the grate with the olive oil.

2. Dust a clean work surface with the flour, and divide the dough in half. Roll each portion of dough out to form a 12-inch round. Transfer one of the dough rounds to a pizza peel, or the back of a large baking sheet, coated with cornmeal. Slide the dough onto the hot grill and cook, without turning, until it is well marked and cooked on one side, about 3 minutes. Turn the dough over and quickly spread half of the pesto over the dough in a thin, even layer. Lay half of the prosciutto slices over the pesto, and then sprinkle half of the cheese evenly over the prosciutto. Continue to cook, rotating the dough every 30 seconds or so, until the cheese is melted and the bottom of the crust is well marked and cooked through, 3 to 4 minutes.

3. Repeat with the remaining dough, pesto, prosciutto, and cheese.

4. Cut each pizza into 6 slices and serve immediately.

Two 12-inch pizzas, 4 to 6 servings

Basic Pizza Dough

One 1/4-ounce packet active dry yeast
1 cup warm water (about 110°F)
Pinch of sugar
1 1/2 teaspoons salt
1 1/2 tablespoons extra-virgin olive oil,
   plus more for coating the bowl
2 1/2 to 3 cups all-purpose flour,
   or more if needed

1. Combine the yeast, water, and sugar in a large bowl, and stir well to combine. Set aside until foamy, about 5 minutes.

2. Add the salt, olive oil, and 1 1/2 cups of the flour to the yeast mixture, and mix well to thoroughly combine. Add 1 cup of the remaining flour and mix well with your hands, working to incorporate the flour little by little. The dough should be slightly sticky to the touch. Transfer the dough to a lightly floured work surface and knead it for at least 5 and up to 7 minutes, adding more flour as needed to form a smooth and elastic dough that is not sticky.

3. Lightly oil a 2- or 3-quart bowl, place the dough in it, and turn it to coat it with oil. Cover the bowl with a damp towel and let the dough rise in a warm place until doubled in size, usually at least 1 hour.

Enough for two 12- or 14-inch pizzas

GRILLED VEGETABLE AND GOAT CHEESE SANDWICH

All you need to do is just look at the photo . . . oh, baby. Grill the vegetables ahead of time if you have folks coming over, and for more fun, allow everyone to make their own sandwiches.

1 large globe eggplant,
    ends trimmed, cut into
    1/3-inch-thick rounds

Salt

4 bell peppers of assorted colors

1/2 cup olive oil

2 medium red onions

1 large zucchini, cut on the diagonal
    into 1/3-inch-thick slices

1 large yellow squash, cut on the
    diagonal into 1/3-inch-thick
    slices

Kosher salt and freshly ground
    black pepper

6 ounces soft, mild goat cheese,
    at room temperature

1 1/2 teaspoons minced garlic

2 tablespoons extra-virgin olive oil

3 tablespoons minced fresh basil

1 loaf ciabatta, cut into
    1/2-inch-thick slices

Balsamic Vinaigrette
    (recipe follows)

1. Preheat a grill to medium-high.

2. Place the eggplant slices on a wire rack and sprinkle them lightly with salt on both sides. Set the rack aside until the eggplant begins to "sweat," usually 15 to 20 minutes.

3. Meanwhile, brush all sides of the peppers with some of the olive oil. Grill the peppers, turning them occasionally, until they are blistered and lightly charred on all sides. Place them in a bowl, cover it tightly with plastic wrap, and set it aside to steam while you grill the remaining vegetables.

4. Cut the onions into 1/2-inch-thick rounds, and then insert toothpicks horizontally through the slices to hold them together on the grill. Pat the eggplant slices dry with paper towels. Brush both sides of the eggplant, zucchini, yellow squash, and red onion slices with the remaining olive oil and place them on a large baking sheet or platter. Season with kosher salt and black pepper to taste. Grill the vegetables, in batches if necessary, until they are lightly charred on the edges and nicely marked on both sides, 10 to 15 minutes. Transfer the grilled vegetables to a platter and set it aside.

5. Slide the skins off the bell peppers and discard the cores and seeds. The peppers should separate into nice wide strips. (Rinse the peppers in a little water if necessary to remove any excess charred skin.) Add the peppers to the platter with the other vegetables.

6. In a small bowl, combine the goat cheese, garlic, extra-virgin olive oil, and basil, and stir until well combined. Season to taste with kosher salt and black pepper.

7. Lightly toast the ciabatta slices, just to warm them through, either on the grill or in a toaster.

8. Assemble a sandwich by drizzling some of the vinaigrette over one side of a slice of ciabatta and generously spreading some of the goat cheese mixture over one side of a second slice. Arrange an assortment of grilled vegetables over the vinaigrette-coated slice, and then drizzle with more vinaigrette if desired. Top the mound of vegetables with the second slice of bread, goat cheese side down, and press gently to form a sandwich. Cut it in half. Repeat with the remaining bread, vinaigrette, cheese mixture, and veggies. Serve immediately. (Any unused grilled vegetables can be stored in an airtight container in the refrigerator for up to 4 days. Use them in sandwiches or salads.)

6 to 8 sandwiches, depending on the size of the ciabatta

Balsamic Vinaigrette

¼ cup balsamic vinegar
½ cup extra-virgin olive oil
½ teaspoon sugar
½ teaspoon minced garlic
Kosher salt and freshly ground black pepper

Whisk the vinegar, olive oil, sugar, and garlic together in a small bowl. Season to taste with kosher salt and pepper. **¾ cup**

BURGERS
AND
Kebabs

VENISON SAUSAGE BURGERS

You hunters out there, this is a great way to use venison. The patties can also be made ahead and then frozen until you're ready to use them.

. . . .

1 pound ground lean venison

1 pound fresh pork sausage, casings removed

1/4 cup finely chopped green onion tops

2 teaspoons minced garlic

2 teaspoons Worcestershire sauce

1 teaspoon salt

1/2 teaspoon freshly ground black pepper

6 hamburger buns

Condiments for serving as desired, such as mayonnaise, mustard, shredded lettuce, sliced tomato, sliced onion, or cheese

Spicy Homemade Ketchup, for serving (page 77)

1. Preheat a grill to medium-high.

2. Combine all the ingredients except the buns and the condiments in a bowl and mix gently but thoroughly. Divide the mixture into 6 equal portions and form them into patties. Grill the burgers for 4 to 5 minutes on each side, or until all pink disappears. Place the buns on the grill, cut sides down, and cook until they are just warmed through and lightly toasted, about 30 seconds. Remove the patties and buns from the grill, and place them on serving plates. Garnish with your choice of condiments, and serve immediately.

6 servings

SPICY HOMEMADE KETCHUP

Man, is this good—simple and delicious. You'll want to keep a batch of this ketchup in a mason jar in your refrigerator. Use it in place of regular ketchup on just about anything you can imagine.

3 pounds very ripe tomatoes, coarsely chopped

1½ teaspoons vegetable oil

1 small onion, finely chopped

1 large clove garlic, minced

¼ cup light brown sugar

½ teaspoon dry mustard

½ teaspoon ground ginger

¼ teaspoon crushed red pepper

¼ teaspoon cayenne pepper

¼ teaspoon ground allspice

⅛ teaspoon ground cloves

Pinch of ground cinnamon

¼ cup cider vinegar

Salt to taste

1. Puree the tomatoes in a blender until smooth. Strain the puree through a medium-mesh sieve into a bowl, pressing with a rubber spatula to extract all of the juices. Discard any solids. Set the tomato puree aside.

2. Heat the oil in a nonreactive saucepan over medium-high heat. Add the onion and cook until softened, 3 to 4 minutes (do not allow it to color). Add the tomato puree and all the remaining ingredients except the vinegar and salt, and bring to a boil. Reduce the heat to a simmer and cook, stirring occasionally at the beginning and more often toward the end of the cooking time, for about 1 hour or until thickened. Add the vinegar and season lightly with salt. Cook until the sauce has a ketchup consistency, 25 to 30 minutes longer. Set it aside to cool. Add more salt, if needed.

3. Store the ketchup in an airtight nonreactive container in the refrigerator for up to 1 week.

About 2 cups

VIETNAMESE BBQ PORK MEATBALLS

Boy, are these Vietnamese-inspired meatballs good. Although they are more traditionally served sliced on top of noodle salads or in po'boys, they make great kebabs and feature nicely when served as part of a mixed grill. They are good on their own, but a dip or dollop of the Kicked-Up Vietnamese-Style Mayonnaise takes them to a whole other level.

1½ pounds boneless lean pork, such as loin, trimmed of any gristle or membranes and cut into small dice

½ cup finely chopped shallots

¼ cup sliced green onion tops

3 tablespoons minced garlic

1 tablespoon plus 2 teaspoons sugar

3 tablespoons Vietnamese fish sauce (nuoc nam)

1 tablespoon soy sauce

1 teaspoon Asian chili-garlic sauce

1½ teaspoons freshly ground black pepper

5 tablespoons short-grain glutinous rice, such as sushi rice or Arborio

4 ounces pork fat, cubed

Vegetable oil, as needed

Six to eight 8-inch bamboo skewers, soaked in warm water for at least 30 minutes

Kicked-Up Vietnamese-Style Mayonnaise (recipe follows), optional

1. In a small bowl, combine the pork, shallots, green onion tops, garlic, sugar, fish sauce, soy sauce, chili-garlic sauce, and black pepper. Stir well to combine. Cover and refrigerate for at least 1 hour, or up to overnight.

2. Transfer the meatball mixture to the freezer and chill it for 30 minutes, or until the mixture is partially frozen.

3. Place the rice in a small skillet and heat it over medium-high heat, stirring constantly, until the rice is toasted, golden brown, and fragrant, 6 to 7 minutes. Transfer the rice to a plate and let it cool.

4. When the rice has cooled, place it in a clean coffee grinder or spice mill, and process it to a fine powder. Measure out 3 tablespoons of the powder and set it aside. (Save any remaining powder for another purpose or discard it.)

5. Transfer the partially frozen meat mixture to a food processor, and process to form a completely smooth but stiff paste. Add the pork fat to the processor and process until smooth or finely chopped. Add the roasted rice powder, and pulse several times to combine the mixture. Be careful not to overprocess or the mixture will become sticky.

6. Preheat a grill to medium-low.

7. Transfer the meat mixture to a small bowl. Lightly oil your hands. Divide the meat mixture into heaping 1½ tablespoonfuls, and roll each one into a smooth ball, recoating your hands with oil as necessary. Thread the meatballs onto the bamboo skewers, fitting as many as you can on each skewer.

8. Coat the grill grate lightly with oil, and grill the skewered meatballs, turning the skewers occasionally, until cooked through, about 15 minutes. Serve warm or at room temperature, with the Kicked-Up Vietnamese-Style Mayonnaise for dipping, if desired.

About 32 meatballs, 4 to 6 servings

Kicked-Up Vietnamese-Style Mayonnaise

This spicy mayo is kicked up with Southeast Asia's Sriracha chili sauce. It will add a little spice to any dish and pairs especially well with the Vietnamese meatballs. You can also use it as a spread for the Vietnamese-Style Grilled Pork Po'boy on page 63.

½ cup mayonnaise
1 tablespoon Sriracha sauce
1 teaspoon freshly squeezed lime juice
½ teaspoon chopped fresh cilantro
¼ teaspoon Vietnamese fish sauce (nuoc nam)

Combine all the ingredients in a nonreactive bowl and stir to blend. Serve immediately, or store in an airtight container in the refrigerator for up to 2 days. **⅔ cup**

GREEK-STYLE LAMB KEBABS

These lamb kebabs are tasty little devils, let me tell you . . . and top them with the Feta Spread for something really out of this world! If you're in the mood for something a little more adventurous than simple pitas, try serving these with the Grilled Green Onion Flatbread on page 59. You can cook them both on the grill at the same time. Oh, yeah, baby!

1½ cups finely chopped onion

1 tablespoon grated lemon zest

¼ cup freshly squeezed
  lemon juice

¼ cup chopped fresh parsley

¼ cup chopped fresh cilantro

3 tablespoons chopped fresh mint

2 teaspoons salt

1 teaspoon ground cumin

1 teaspoon sweet paprika

1 teaspoon freshly ground
  black pepper

¼ cup olive oil

2 to 2½ pounds boneless leg
  or shoulder of lamb,
  cut into 1-inch cubes
  (with some of the fat still
  attached)

8 to 10 bamboo skewers

8 pita breads, warmed,
  for serving

Feta Spread (page 95),
  for serving

1. In a large bowl, combine the onion, lemon zest, lemon juice, parsley, cilantro, mint, salt, cumin, paprika, pepper, and olive oil. Stir well. Add the lamb and toss to coat it with the marinade. Cover with plastic wrap and refrigerate for 2 to 4 hours.

2. Soak the skewers in warm water for about 1 hour before assembling the kebabs.

3. Preheat a grill to high, and lightly oil the grate.

4. Thread the lamb onto the soaked skewers, and place them on the grill. Cook, turning frequently to promote even browning, for 12 to 14 minutes.

5. Wrap a pita bread around the meat on a skewer, and while holding the bread firmly around the meat, twist the skewer out of the meat. Drizzle the meat with Feta Spread to your liking. Repeat with the remaining pitas and skewers, and enjoy!

6 to 8 servings

HOME-GROUND BURGERS WITH BACON, CHEESE, AND FRESH THYME

Ahhhh man, are these terrific! How can you go wrong with bacon and cheese? Make sure you use chuck that is not too lean; you really need about 15 percent fat for the perfect burger. These burgers are *big*—if you're not up to the size, simply shape the mixture into smaller patties and make sure to adjust the cook time accordingly. If you're a ketchup-lover like me, try the Orange Habanero Ketchup on page 85 on these babies. You'll be amazed.

2 pounds boneless beef chuck, cut into 1-inch cubes

6 ounces bacon, chopped

1 cup finely chopped onion

3 tablespoons thinly sliced garlic

1 tablespoon fresh thyme leaves

2 tablespoons Worcestershire sauce

1 teaspoon salt

1/2 teaspoon freshly ground black pepper

8 slices cheddar cheese

4 sesame-seed hamburger rolls, lightly toasted

1 1/2 cups shredded iceberg lettuce

8 thin slices tomato

Mayonnaise, for serving

Ketchup, for serving

Mustard, for serving

Pickles, for serving

1. Place the diced chuck in a large bowl.

2. Set a 10-inch sauté pan over medium heat and add the bacon. Cook, stirring occasionally, until the bacon is crisp and most of the fat has been rendered, 7 to 8 minutes. Add the onions to the pan and cook until they are softened, 4 to 5 minutes. Add the garlic and cook until fragrant, 1 minute longer. Add the thyme and toss to combine. Remove the pan from the heat and pour the mixture over the diced chuck. Drizzle with the Worcestershire, and season with the salt and pepper. Toss gently but thoroughly to combine. Cover and set aside to marinate, refrigerated, for 1 hour.

3. Assemble a home grinder according to the manufacturer's instructions, using a medium die for grinding. Grind the meat mixture and then gently form it into 4 patties, being careful not to overwork it. Cover and refrigerate until chilled, about 1 hour.

4. Preheat a grill to medium, and lightly oil the grate.

5. Remove the patties from the refrigerator and place them on the grill. Cook for 7 to 8 minutes. Then turn them over and place 2 slices of the cheddar on each burger. Cook for another 7 to 8 minutes for medium-rare to medium, or until the burgers are cooked to the desired degree of doneness. Place a burger on the bottom of each of the 4 toasted buns. Dress with the lettuce and tomatoes, and add mayo, ketchup, mustard, and pickles as desired. Serve immediately.

4 servings

ORANGE HABANERO KETCHUP

Talk about kicked up a notch. I love the spice here! It's just right.

2 tablespoons olive oil

3/4 cup finely chopped onion

1 habanero chile, stemmed
   and seeded

1 1/2 teaspoons minced garlic

1 tablespoon minced fresh ginger

1/2 cup red wine vinegar

1/2 cup cider vinegar

1 cup packed dark brown sugar

3/4 cup freshly squeezed
   orange juice

2 teaspoons grated orange zest

1 teaspoon kosher salt

1/2 teaspoon ground mustard

1/4 teaspoon ground mace

One 28-ounce can whole plum
   tomatoes, with their juices,
   broken into pieces

1. Set a 2-quart saucepan over medium heat and add the olive oil. Once the oil is hot, add the onions, habanero, garlic, and ginger and cook until softened, 4 to 5 minutes. Add the wine vinegar, cider vinegar, brown sugar, orange juice, orange zest, kosher salt, mustard, and mace. Stir to combine. Bring the sauce to a boil, and add the tomatoes and tomato juices. Continue to cook until the liquid has reduced by half, 20 to 25 minutes.

2. Remove the pan from the heat and set it aside to cool briefly. Then transfer the mixture to a food processor, and puree until very smooth. Serve at room temperature or slightly chilled.

3. Store the ketchup in a clean nonreactive container in the refrigerator for up to 3 weeks.

About 3 cups

SPICED BUFFALO BURGERS

I've come to really love a good buffalo burger. If you've not yet tried one, I suggest you give it a whirl. The full, rich flavor is to die for, and as an added bonus, the meat is naturally lean.

2 pounds ground buffalo

3 tablespoons Worcestershire sauce

1 tablespoon Chile Spice Blend for Burgers (recipe follows)

2 tablespoons vegetable or olive oil

1 small onion, cut into ½-inch-thick rounds

Shredded cheddar or Swiss cheese (optional)

6 hamburger buns

Mayonnaise, for serving

Sliced pickles, for serving

Red-leaf lettuce, for serving

Tomato slices, for serving

1. Cover a baking sheet with aluminum foil or waxed paper, and set it aside.

2. Place the meat in a large mixing bowl. Add the Worcestershire and the Chile Spice Blend, and mix gently but thoroughly with your hands until all the ingredients are well incorporated. Form the meat into 6 equal patties, placing them on the prepared baking sheet as they are formed.

3. Preheat a grill to medium-high. Lightly oil the grate with some of the oil.

4. Brush the onion slices with the remaining oil. Grill the onion slices, turning them occasionally, until lightly caramelized, 6 to 8 minutes. Remove them from the heat and set them aside until ready to serve the burgers.

5. Place the buffalo patties on the grill and cook for 6 to 8 minutes. Turn the burgers over, place the cheese on the patties if using, and top the patties with the bun top. Cook on the second side for 2 to 3 minutes. Place the bun bottoms, cut side down, on the grill briefly to toast.

6. Arrange the bun bottoms on a large platter, cut side up. Top with the desired condiments. Slide the patties and the bun tops onto the bun bottoms. Serve with the grilled onions.

6 servings

Chile Spice Blend for Burgers

2 teaspoons ancho chili powder
$1/2$ teaspoon ground cumin
$1/2$ teaspoon chipotle powder
$1/2$ teaspoon chili powder
$1/2$ teaspoon dried oregano
$1/2$ teaspoon salt
$1/4$ teaspoon freshly ground black pepper

Combine all the ingredients in a small bowl and stir to blend. Store the spice blend in an airtight container until ready to use. It will keep up to 6 months in a dark, cool place. **About 3 table-spoons**

GRILLED SWORDFISH KEBABS WITH MIXED HERB PESTO

This is a great way to showcase swordfish, a fish that's right at home on the grill and especially nice when served with seasonal local veggies. The mixed herb pesto is so delicious, it's good on just about anything.

1¾ to 2 pounds 1-inch-thick swordfish steaks, cut into 1½-inch cubes

1 red bell pepper, stemmed, seeded, and cut into 1-inch pieces

1 yellow bell pepper, stemmed, seeded, and cut into 1-inch pieces

1 red onion, cut into ½-inch-thick lengthwise slices

One 6-inch-long zucchini, halved lengthwise and cut into ½-inch-thick slices

16 cremini mushrooms, stems trimmed

8 long (11- to 12-inch) skewers (if using wooden skewers, soak them in warm water for at least 15 minutes)

⅓ cup extra-virgin olive oil

¾ teaspoon salt

½ teaspoon freshly ground black pepper

Mixed Herb Pesto (recipe follows)

1. Preheat a grill or broiler to high.

2. Assemble the kebabs by dividing the swordfish and vegetables evenly among the skewers, alternating colors and ingredients. Lightly brush all sides of each filled skewer with the olive oil, and then season the skewers with the salt and pepper. Grill or broil the skewers 6 inches from the heat source until the fish is just cooked through and the vegetables are lightly browned on the edges, about 8 minutes.

3. Enjoy while hot, with some of the Mixed Herb Pesto drizzled over all.

8 appetizer servings or 4 main-course servings

Mixed Herb Pesto

1 cup fresh basil leaves
1 cup fresh parsley leaves
1/2 cup fresh mint leaves
1/4 cup fresh cilantro leaves
1/4 cup chopped fresh chives
1/2 cup pine nuts, lightly toasted
4 cloves garlic, minced
1/2 cup freshly grated Parmesan cheese
1 cup extra-virgin olive oil
2 teaspoons freshly squeezed lemon juice
1 teaspoon salt
1/4 teaspoon freshly ground black pepper

Combine the basil, parsley, mint, cilantro, and chives in a food processor and process until finely chopped. Add the pine nuts, garlic, and Parmesan cheese, and with the machine running, add the oil in a thin, steady stream. Add the lemon juice, salt, and pepper, and pulse to combine. Transfer the pesto to a nonreactive bowl and cover it with plastic wrap, pressing the wrap so that it sits directly on top of the pesto. Set aside until ready to use.

Note: The pesto sauce can be made up to 2 days in advance and refrigerated until ready to use. If you choose to make it ahead of time, cover the surface of the sauce with a thin film of olive oil to keep the sauce from darkening. Return it to room temperature before serving. **1²/₃ cups**

PORK AND CHORIZO BURGERS WITH GREEN CHILE MAYO

Chorizo, pork, and green chiles come together to form one killer burger here. Try these at your next tailgating party and watch 'em come back for more. If you happen to have any of the Green Chile Mayonnaise left over, don't worry—it tastes great on lots of things. Slather it on sandwiches, spread it over ears of hot grilled corn, use it in dips, you name it!

8 ounces chorizo, casings removed, cut into 1-inch pieces

1½ pounds ground pork

1 tablespoon minced garlic

2 teaspoons Worcestershire sauce

1½ teaspoons Emeril's Original Essence or Creole Seasoning (page 25)

¾ teaspoon salt

¼ teaspoon cayenne pepper

4 large hamburger buns, or four 6-inch lengths French bread, split in half horizontally

1 cup coarsely grated Pepper Jack cheese (optional)

Green Chile Mayo (recipe follows)

1. Preheat a grill to medium-high.

2. Place the chorizo in a food processor and process until finely chopped (the sausage should appear crumbly). Transfer the chorizo to a large bowl and add the ground pork, garlic, Worcestershire, Original Essence, salt, and cayenne. Mix gently but thoroughly, being careful not to overwork the mixture. Form the mixture into four 1-inch-thick patties, about 8 ounces each, and place them on the grill. Cook to a minimum internal temperature of 160°F, 5 to 7 minutes per side. During the last 2 minutes of grilling, toast the buns, and if desired, sprinkle the cheese over the tops of the burgers and cook until melted.

3. Place the burgers on the bun bottoms and set them on plates. Generously top each burger with 2 tablespoons of the Green Chile Mayo, and place the tops of the buns over the sauce. Serve immediately.

Note: These are *big* burgers! If you like, form them into smaller patties for an audience with dainty appetites, but please adjust the cook time accordingly.

4 servings

Green Chile Mayo

1 cup good-quality mayonnaise
  (preferably homemade)
1 teaspoon minced garlic
1 poblano chile, roasted, peeled,
  and seeded
1 tablespoon freshly squeezed lime juice
Salt and freshly ground black pepper to taste

Combine the mayonnaise, garlic, poblano, and lime juice in a food processor, and process until smooth. Season to taste with salt and pepper. This keeps up to 1 week. **About 1½ cups**

LAMB BURGERS WITH FETA SPREAD

I've been making these burgers for years, and folks just love 'em. Feel free to adjust the spices to suit your taste; sometimes I like to add a little garam masala to move in a slightly different direction.

2¼ pounds ground lamb
   (10 percent fat content)

½ cup minced shallots

3 tablespoons minced fresh mint

1 tablespoon minced garlic

1½ teaspoons salt

½ teaspoon ground cumin

¼ teaspoon ground allspice

¼ teaspoon cayenne pepper

¼ teaspoon ground cinnamon

1 tablespoon olive oil

6 hamburger buns

Feta Spread (recipe follows),
   for serving

Lettuce leaves, for garnish
   (optional)

Thinly sliced tomatoes, for garnish
   (optional)

Sliced roasted red peppers,
   for garnish (optional)

1. In a mixing bowl, combine the lamb, shallots, mint, garlic, salt, cumin, allspice, cayenne, and cinnamon. Mix gently but thoroughly to combine. Using your hands, shape the mixture into 6 wide patties about ½ inch thick, and transfer them to a large plate or a platter. Cover with plastic wrap and refrigerate for at least 2 hours or up to overnight.

2. When you are ready to cook the burgers, preheat a grill to medium-high.

3. Brush both sides of the burgers with the olive oil. When the grill is hot, add the burgers and cook for about 4 minutes on each side for medium. Transfer the burgers to a platter and cover loosely with foil. Place the buns, cut side down, and in batches if necessary, on the grill and cook until warmed through and lightly toasted, 1 to 2 minutes.

4. Place the burgers on the buns, and spoon some of the Feta Spread over each burger. Garnish with lettuce, tomatoes, and sliced roasted peppers if desired, and serve immediately.

6 servings

Feta Spread

4 ounces feta cheese, crumbled
4 ounces cream cheese,
    at room temperature
$1/2$ cup Greek-style yogurt
2 tablespoons minced green onion tops
1 tablespoon minced fresh mint
2 teaspoons freshly squeezed lemon juice
$1^1/2$ teaspoons minced garlic
1 teaspoon olive oil
1 teaspoon finely grated lemon zest
$1/2$ teaspoon salt, or more to taste
    (depending on the saltiness of the feta)
$1/8$ teaspoon cayenne pepper

Combine all the ingredients in a bowl, and stir to
blend well. Cover with plastic wrap and refrigerate
for at least 1 hour or up to overnight to allow the
flavors to blend. **About 2 cups**

RIB-EYE, NEW POTATO, AND PORTOBELLO KEBABS ON ROSEMARY SKEWERS

I just love the deep, earthy flavor of portobellos. Combining them with new potatoes and large chunks of rib-eye, and infusing it all with an intense rosemary flavor, makes these skewers irresistible!

4 new potatoes, such as Red Bliss (about 3 ounces each)

1 large portobello mushroom cap (about 4 ounces)

One 14- to 16-ounce rib-eye steak

1½ teaspoons sea salt

½ teaspoon freshly ground black pepper

⅓ cup extra-virgin olive oil

⅓ cup balsamic vinegar

2 tablespoons chopped fresh rosemary

2 tablespoons minced garlic

Four 10- to 12-inch-long thick, woody rosemary branches, or four 12-inch bamboo skewers, soaked in warm water for at least 30 minutes

1. Place the potatoes in a 1-quart saucepan and add water to cover by 1 inch. Set the pan over high heat and bring to a boil. Reduce the heat and cook the potatoes at a gentle boil for 10 minutes, or until barely fork-tender. Drain, and allow the potatoes to cool. They should be cool enough to handle. Then cut the potatoes in half and set them aside until ready to use.

2. Remove the stem and gills from the portobello with a sharp knife, and cut the cap into 8 wedges. Place the wedges in a medium bowl.

3. Cut the steak into 8 equal pieces, about 1¾ to 2 ounces each, and season them with ½ teaspoon of the sea salt and the black pepper. Place the meat in the bowl with the mushrooms. Add the olive oil, balsamic vinegar, chopped rosemary, and garlic, and stir to coat the mushrooms and steak well. Cover the bowl with plastic wrap and marinate in the refrigerator for 30 minutes or up to 2 hours.

4. Heat a grill to medium-high, and lightly oil the grate.

5. Remove the bowl from the refrigerator. Skewer a potato on a rosemary branch, followed by a piece of steak and a mushroom wedge. Add another potato, piece of steak, and mushroom wedge. Repeat with the remaining skewers. Reserve any marinade remaining in the bowl for basting the skewers as they cook.

6. Grill the kebabs, basting them with the remaining marinade as they cook, for about 3 minutes. Turn and cook for another 3 minutes, basting, before turning them over to cook on the first side again. Continue to cook on the first side for 2 to 3 minutes before turning them over and cooking a final 2 to 3 minutes. Season the kebabs with the remaining 1 teaspoon sea salt, and serve immediately.

4 servings

SOUTHWESTERN TURKEY SLIDERS

If your family is like mine, you have at least one "I only eat turkey burgers" among the ranks. Serve these up at your next family gathering and see both meat eaters and non meat eaters enjoy them. The secret to keeping the turkey burgers moist lies in using a blend of turkey breast meat and thigh meat for the best flavor and texture. Be careful not to overcook these beauties.

2 pounds ground turkey, preferably a blend of thigh and breast meat

1/2 cup minced red onion

1/4 cup minced green onion, white and green parts

1 or 2 serrano chiles, to taste, minced

2 egg whites, whisked

1 1/2 tablespoons Emeril's Southwest Essence spice blend

1 teaspoon ground cumin

1 tablespoon Worcestershire sauce

12 mini burger buns or small soft dinner rolls, warmed

1 cup grated cheddar cheese

12 small lettuce leaves

12 slices tomato

1 cup thinly sliced red onions

1 avocado, peeled, pitted, and thinly sliced

Mayonnaise (optional)

Mustard (optional)

Ketchup (optional)

1. Preheat a grill to medium-high.

2. In a large bowl, combine the ground turkey with the minced red onion, green onion, chile, egg whites, Southwest Essence, cumin, and Worcestershire. Mix gently but thoroughly. Divide the mixture into 12 equal portions, and using your hands, shape them into 12 small burgers, each about 3 1/2 inches wide.

3. Place the burgers on the grill and cook until the turkey is just done and an instant-read thermometer inserted into the center registers 165°F, about 3 minutes per side.

4. Serve the burgers on the mini buns, topped with the cheese, lettuce, tomato, sliced red onion, and avocado. Garnish with mayonnaise, mustard, and ketchup to your liking.

12 sliders, 6 servings

SIRLOIN SLIDERS WITH CRISP BACON AND CREAMY HORSERADISH MAYO

These tasty little babies are just right for grilling get-togethers where you have other dishes sharing the limelight. Since they're petite, they grill up quickly—but, boy, do they pack a lot of flavor. If you can't find small brioche hamburger buns, simply substitute small dinner rolls or potato rolls.

12 ounces ground beef chuck

12 ounces ground sirloin

2 teaspoons minced garlic

1/4 cup minced onion

1 1/4 teaspoons salt

1/2 teaspoon plus 1/8 teaspoon freshly ground black pepper

1/2 cup mayonnaise

2 tablespoons sour cream

3 tablespoons prepared horseradish

12 dinner-roll-size brioche buns, split in half

2 tablespoons butter, melted

6 slices bacon, cooked until crisp, drained, and broken into 2-inch pieces

1. In a mixing bowl, combine the chuck, sirloin, garlic, onion, 1 teaspoon of the salt, and the 1/2 teaspoon pepper. Mix gently but thoroughly to combine. Using a 2-ounce ice cream scoop or a 1/4 cup measure, divide the mixture into 12 portions. Using your hands, shape them to form small patties, about 3 inches wide and 3/8 inch thick. Place the patties on a plate, cover with plastic wrap, and refrigerate for at least 1 hour or up to overnight for the flavors to mingle.

2. In a small nonreactive bowl, whisk together the mayonnaise, sour cream, and horseradish. Season the mixture with the remaining 1/4 teaspoon salt and 1/8 teaspoon pepper. Cover and refrigerate until ready to serve (the mayo can be prepared up to 3 days in advance).

3. When you are ready to cook the burgers, preheat a grill to high.

4. Lightly brush the cut sides of the buns with the melted butter. Wrap the buns in aluminum foil and place them on the coolest part of the grill to warm while you cook the burgers.

5. Grill the burgers for about 2 minutes per side for medium. Transfer the burgers to the bottom portions of the warmed buns, and garnish with the pieces of crisp bacon. Spoon a dollop of the horseradish mayonnaise over the bacon, then place the bun tops over all. Serve the sliders hot.

12 sliders, 4 to 6 servings

FROM
the Sea

LOBSTER TAILS WITH LEMON-TARRAGON BUTTER

This is a great way to cook lobster when you feel like being outside and you want something a little different from the same-old same-old. Grilling really brings out the inherent sweetness of lobster. And hey, if you happen to not like the flavor of tarragon, don't worry! Simply substitute an herb that you do enjoy, such as chives or basil.

Two live lobsters
(about 1½ pounds each)

4 tablespoons (½ stick)
unsalted butter

1 teaspoon grated lemon zest

1 tablespoon freshly squeezed
lemon juice

¼ teaspoon plus a pinch of salt

⅛ teaspoon plus a pinch of freshly
ground white pepper

1 tablespoon chopped fresh
tarragon, plus more for garnish
(optional)

2 tablespoons olive oil

1. Fill a 2- to 3-gallon stockpot with water and bring it to a boil over high heat. Once the water comes to a boil, immerse the lobsters in the pot and cook them for 3 minutes. Remove the lobsters and immediately chill them in an ice bath. Once the lobsters are cool enough to handle, remove them from the water and place them on a kitchen towel draped over a cutting board.

2. Twist the tails off the lobsters. Using a large chef's knife, score along the length of each tail and then cut each tail in half lengthwise. Set the cut tails aside. Crack the shells of the claws, remove the meat, and reserve it for another use (such as pasta or a salad).

3. Set a small saucepan over low heat and add the butter, lemon zest, and lemon juice. Bring to a gentle simmer and cook for 3 to 4 minutes, allowing the flavors to infuse. Season with the pinch of salt, pinch of white pepper, and tarragon.

4. Preheat a grill to medium-high.

5. Brush the cut sides of the lobster tails with the olive oil, and season them with the remaining ¼ teaspoon salt and ⅛ teaspoon white pepper. Place the tails, cut side down, on the grill, and cook for 3 minutes. Rotate the tails 90 degrees and cook for an additional 3 minutes. Turn the lobster tails over and cook for 2 minutes longer.

6. Place the lobster tails on a platter or serving plates. Drizzle the lemon-tarragon butter over them, and garnish with additional tarragon if desired. Serve immediately.

2 main-course or 4 appetizer servings

SWORDFISH WITH CIDER VINAIGRETTE AND AN APPLE-ENDIVE SLAW

The crisp texture of this apple and endive slaw atop a piece of simply grilled swordfish is an exercise in elegance.

¼ cup cider vinegar

1 tablespoon minced shallots

2 teaspoons honey

½ teaspoon minced garlic

½ teaspoon Dijon mustard

½ cup extra-virgin olive oil

1¼ teaspoons salt

1¼ teaspoons freshly ground white pepper

2 heads Belgian endive, spears separated and julienned (about 3 cups)

1 Golden Delicious or Fuji apple, cored and julienned

½ cup toasted and roughly chopped hazelnuts

⅓ cup thinly sliced celery

¼ cup roughly chopped fresh parsley

2 tablespoons fresh tarragon leaves

½ teaspoon freshly ground black pepper

Six 6-ounce swordfish steaks

2 tablespoons olive oil

2 teaspoons kosher salt

1. Combine the vinegar, shallots, honey, garlic, and mustard in a medium bowl, and whisk well to combine. Then, while whisking constantly, slowly drizzle in the extra-virgin olive oil to form a lightly emulsified vinaigrette. Season the vinaigrette with ½ teaspoon of the salt and ¼ teaspoon of the white pepper. Set it aside.

2. In another medium bowl, combine the endive, apple, hazelnuts, celery, parsley, tarragon, the remaining ¾ teaspoon salt, the black pepper, and 6 tablespoons of the vinaigrette. Toss the ingredients well, and set the slaw aside.

3. Preheat a grill to medium-high, and oil the grate.

4. Rub the swordfish steaks with the olive oil, and season them with the kosher salt and the remaining 1 teaspoon white pepper. Place the swordfish on the grill and cook for 2½ minutes. Rotate the fish 90 degrees and cook for an additional 2½ minutes. Turn the fish over and cook for 2 to 4 minutes, or until it is just cooked through. Transfer the swordfish to a platter, and spoon the apple-endive slaw over the top. Drizzle the remaining vinaigrette around the fish, and serve immediately.

6 servings

SALMON WITH PEACH-TAMARIND BARBECUE SAUCE

I particularly love the flavor of salmon cooked on the grill. And oh, with this Peach-Tamarind Barbecue Sauce! If you're lucky enough to have any sauce left over, it's great on grilled chicken or ribs.

2 tablespoons unsalted butter

1/2 cup diced red onion

1 teaspoon minced garlic

1 serrano chile, stemmed, halved, and thinly sliced

4 cups peeled, pitted, and diced peaches, or 4 cups frozen diced peaches, thawed

1/2 cup ketchup

1/4 cup fresh orange juice

1/2 teaspoon grated orange zest

2 tablespoons cider vinegar

2 to 3 tablespoons light brown sugar

2 teaspoons tamarind paste

1 teaspoon salt

1/2 teaspoon freshly ground black pepper

Four 6-ounce pieces salmon fillet, skin removed

1 tablespoon olive oil

1. Melt the butter in a medium saucepan over medium heat. Add the onion and cook, stirring occasionally, until translucent, about 5 minutes. Stir in the garlic and serrano chile (with the seeds), and cook, stirring, for 2 minutes. Add the peaches and cook until softened, about 5 minutes. Add the ketchup, orange juice, orange zest, vinegar, brown sugar, and tamarind paste, and stir to combine. Bring the mixture to a simmer and cook for 30 minutes, or until thickened. Using an immersion blender, or transferring the mixture to a regular blender, puree the sauce until smooth. Strain the sauce through a fine-mesh sieve into a bowl, pressing with a rubber spatula to extract all the juices. Discard the solids. Season the sauce with 1/4 teaspoon of the salt and 1/4 teaspoon of the pepper. Allow the sauce to cool to room temperature before serving. (The sauce can be made up to 1 week in advance and stored in an airtight nonreactive container in the fridge. Return it to room temperature before serving.)

2. Preheat a grill to medium.

3. Brush the salmon on both sides with the olive oil, and season with the remaining 3/4 teaspoon salt and the 1/4 teaspoon pepper. Place the fish on the grill and cook for about 2 minutes. Then rotate the fish 45 degrees and cook for an additional 2 minutes. Turn the fish over, and cook for 2 minutes, or until cooked to the desired degree of doneness.

4. Serve the salmon drizzled with the Peach-Tamarind Barbecue Sauce.

4 servings

CHIPOTLE BBQ OYSTERS WITH HOMEMADE SALSA FRESCA

This dish is definitely an inspiration from New Orleans' famous Drago's Restaurant. That and the countless times I've been invited to outdoor grilling events and someone would show up with a sack of oysters, an oyster knife, and a bottle of barbecue sauce . . . Here's my take on what to do with 'em.

48 fresh oysters in their shells, scrubbed well under cold running water

Chipotle BBQ Sauce (recipe follows)

Homemade Salsa Fresca (recipe follows)

1. Preheat a grill to high.

2. Shuck the oysters and discard the top, flatter shells. (Loosen the oysters from the bottom shells by running the oyster knife carefully underneath the body of each oyster.) Return each oyster to its bottom, deeper shell. Place the oysters on the grill, shell side down, and cook until the oysters begin to curl around the edges, 2 to 3 minutes. Carefully spoon about a teaspoon of the Chipotle BBQ Sauce over each oyster, and continue to grill until the oysters are just cooked through and the sauce is bubbly around the edges, about 2 minutes longer. Transfer the oysters to a platter or to serving plates, and top each one with a teaspoon of the Salsa Fresca. Serve immediately. (Careful—the shells will be hot!)

4 main-course or 8 appetizer servings

Chipotle BBQ Sauce

1/2 cup sugar
1/4 cup cider vinegar
2 tablespoons tomato paste
1 tablespoon dark Asian sesame oil
1 tablespoon molasses
1 tablespoon soy sauce
2 teaspoons chopped chipotle chiles in adobo sauce

1. Combine all the ingredients in a small saucepan and bring to a boil. Reduce the heat to medium-low and simmer until the mixture starts to become syrupy and dime-size bubbles form, 12 to 15 minutes. Remove from the heat and allow to cool slightly.

2. Transfer the sauce to a blender or food processor, filling it no more than halfway, and place a towel over the top of the machine. While exercising caution (hot liquids can expand when being processed and force the lid off a blender), pulse a few times; then process on high speed until smooth. This will keep up to 1 month. **About 2/3 cup**

Homemade Salsa Fresca

1 cup peeled and chopped tomatillos or seeded
    chopped tomatoes
1/4 cup freshly squeezed lime juice
1/4 cup minced red onion
2 tablespoons chopped fresh cilantro
1 1/2 teaspoons minced jalapeño
1/2 teaspoon salt
1/8 teaspoon freshly ground black pepper

Combine all the ingredients in a small bowl, and mix together thoroughly. Cover and refrigerate until ready to use. This will keep up to 2 days. **About 1 1/2 cups**

SOFT-SHELL CRABS ON THE GRILL

I could grill soft-shell crabs every day. You've gotta grab them up while they're in season! I like them in po'boys, I like them in salads, I like them dry-marinated—you name it. The simpler, the better, as long as they are fresh. For a real showstopper, I recommend serving these with the Watercress, Avocado, and Mango Salad on page 39.

6 soft-shell crabs

¼ cup olive oil

Salt and freshly ground
    black pepper to taste

1. Rinse the crabs under cold running water and brush them with a small brush if necessary to remove any dirt on their outer shells. Twist off and discard the apron. Fold back the pointed sides of the top shell to expose the gills; remove the gills on both sides. Using kitchen scissors, cut across the front of the crab about ¼ inch behind the eyes and mouth and squeeze out the small sac hiding directly behind the mouth. The crabs are now ready to be cooked.

2. Preheat a grill to medium-high with the lid down.

3. Brush the crabs with some of the olive oil, and season them with salt and pepper. Place the crabs on the grill, cover it, and cook, turning the crabs every few minutes and basting them with the remaining olive oil until they turn orange and are cooked through, 7 to 9 minutes, depending on their size. Remove from the grill, and serve hot.

6 servings

SARDINES PORTUGUESE-STYLE

This dish is straight out of my childhood. I can remember special times when Hilda and Mr. John (my parents) would grill sardines with olive oil and set out lots of crusty Portuguese bread for serving. Yum! Wish I were ten again.

12 to 16 fresh whole sardines (2 to 2½ pounds), scaled, cleaned, and rinsed

2 cups peeled, seeded, and diced tomatoes (small dice; from about 1 pound tomatoes)

¾ cup extra-virgin olive oil

⅓ cup coarsely chopped pitted Kalamata olives

⅓ cup chopped fresh parsley

2 tablespoons chopped fresh basil

2 tablespoons minced red onion

1 tablespoon minced garlic

¼ cup plus 1 tablespoon freshly squeezed lemon juice

Coarse sea salt and freshly ground black pepper

½ cup olive oil

1 lemon, sliced into ⅓-inch-thick rounds

4 Roma tomatoes (about 1 pound), halved

1. Lay the sardines side by side on a clean, dry kitchen towel or on paper towels, and gently roll together into a cylinder to remove excess moisture. Refrigerate until ready to use. (It is very important that the sardines are sufficiently dry before oiling, seasoning, and grilling.)

2. Preheat a very clean, well-oiled grill or broiler to high.

3. In a medium mixing bowl, combine the diced tomatoes, ½ cup of the extra-virgin olive oil, olives, parsley, basil, onion, and garlic. Add the 1 tablespoon lemon juice, 1 teaspoon sea salt, and ½ teaspoon black pepper. Mix well. Set aside at room temperature until you are ready to serve the sardines.

4. Transfer the sardines to a small rimmed baking sheet, and drizzle ¼ cup of the olive oil over them. Turn the sardines in the oil to coat them. Oil the grill grate one more time before you begin cooking. Season the sardines on both sides with 1 teaspoon salt and ½ teaspoon pepper. Place them directly on the grill and cook, undisturbed, until the skin is crispy and lightly charred, 2 to 3 minutes. Turn them over and cook for another 2 to 3 minutes. (If you try to turn the fish too soon, they will stick to the grill. Be patient here and the fish will turn easily once the skin has crisped.)

5. While the fish are cooking, brush the lemon slices and tomato halves lightly with the remaining ¼ cup olive oil. Season them with sea salt and black pepper to taste, and place them on the grill. Grill until softened and nicely marked on both sides, about 2 minutes.

6. Arrange the grilled sardines on a serving platter, season them a final time with sea salt and black pepper, and drizzle with the remaining ¼ cup lemon juice and the remaining ¼ cup extra-virgin olive oil. Serve immediately, with the grilled tomato halves, grilled lemon slices, and tomato-olive vinaigrette spooned over all.

4 servings

SHRIMP WITH GARLIC, LEMON, AND MARJORAM

Those of us who live along the coast of the Gulf of Mexico are truly fortunate to be able to get beautiful fresh shrimp right off the boats when they come in. You don't have to do much to them when they are this fresh.

2 pounds jumbo shrimp, heads removed, peel left on

1 cup olive oil

1/2 cup freshly squeezed lemon juice

2 tablespoons chopped fresh marjoram

2 teaspoons grated lemon zest

2 teaspoons kosher salt

1 teaspoon freshly ground black pepper

1 teaspoon sea salt

1 tablespoon chopped fresh parsley

1 lemon, cut into 6 wedges

1. Use a pair of kitchen shears to cut through the backs of the shrimp, and remove the veins. Place the shrimp in a large bowl.

2. In a medium bowl, combine the olive oil, lemon juice, marjoram, lemon zest, kosher salt, and pepper. Whisk to combine, and then drizzle the marinade over the shrimp. Cover the bowl with plastic wrap and refrigerate it for 2 hours, stirring the shrimp occasionally after the first hour.

3. Preheat a grill to high.

4. Remove the shrimp from the marinade and place them on the grill. Cook for 2 to 3 minutes, or until they are bright pink and lightly marked by the grill on the first side. Turn the shrimp over and cook until just cooked through, 1 to 2 minutes longer. Transfer the shrimp to a large platter, season them with the sea salt, and garnish with the chopped parsley and lemon wedges.

6 servings

SALMON WITH A PINEAPPLE, MANGO, AND STRAWBERRY SALSA

The mixed fruit salsa here is light and refreshing—the perfect accompaniment to grilled fish in the summertime. Try to buy wild-caught salmon and, if possible, get the West Coast variety.

Four 6-ounce pieces of salmon fillet, skin on

4 teaspoons olive oil

2 teaspoons Emeril's Original Essence or Creole Seasoning (page 25)

1 teaspoon salt

1/2 teaspoon freshly ground black pepper

Pineapple, Mango, and Strawberry Salsa (recipe follows)

1. Preheat a grill to medium.

2. Brush both sides of the salmon with the olive oil, and season with the Original Essence, salt, and pepper. Place the fish on the grill, skin side down, and cook for about 3 minutes. Then rotate the fish 45 degrees and cook for an additional 3 minutes. Turn the fish over, and cook for 2 minutes, or until cooked to the desired degree of doneness.

3. Transfer the fish to a platter or individual plates, spoon the fruit salsa over it, and serve immediately.

4 servings

Pineapple, Mango, and Strawberry Salsa

3/4 cup diced pineapple (small dice)
3/4 cup diced mango (small dice)
1/2 cup diced strawberries (small dice)
1/4 cup diced red onion (small dice)
1 jalapeño, stemmed, seeded, and finely chopped
2 tablespoons chopped fresh mint
2 tablespoons freshly squeezed orange juice
1 tablespoon freshly squeezed lime juice
1/4 teaspoon salt

Combine all of the ingredients in a medium nonreactive bowl, and stir to blend. Cover the bowl with plastic wrap, and set it aside until the flavors have married, usually 20 to 30 minutes. **About 2 cups**

ARCTIC CHAR WITH A PEAR BUTTER SAUCE

This dish is a knockout—the deep, rich flavor of arctic char paired with a sweet, creamy pear sauce. It's a nice dish to make in early fall, when it's still warm enough to sneak out to the grill and when pears are just coming into season. But, hey, if you live where the temperatures drop quickly in the fall, simply break out a grill pan and bring the grilling life indoors. Try serving this with roasted fingerling potatoes or the Grilled Smashed Potatoes on page 20.

2 firm-ripe pears, such as Bartlett, peeled, cored, and diced

2 tablespoons packed light brown sugar

1/2 cup hard cider

1/2 cup heavy cream

16 tablespoons (2 sticks) cold unsalted butter, cut into pieces

3 tablespoons olive oil

Four 6-ounce pieces arctic char fillet, skin on

Salt and freshly ground white pepper

1. To make the pear butter sauce, combine the diced pears, brown sugar, and hard cider in a medium saucepan. Cook over medium-high heat until the pears are translucent, about 5 minutes. Add the cream and cook until reduced by half, about 6 minutes. Add the butter, several pieces at a time, whisking constantly to blend and removing the pan from the heat periodically to prevent the sauce from breaking. (Do not allow the sauce to boil or it will separate.) Add 1/4 teaspoon salt and 1/8 teaspoon white pepper, and whisk to blend. Remove from the heat and cover to keep warm until ready to serve, stirring occasionally.

2. Preheat a well-oiled grill to medium-high.

3. Season both sides of each fillet with salt and white pepper to taste, and place the fish on the grill. Grill until the center is still slightly pink, rotating the fish 90 degrees halfway through cooking to form nice grill marks, 3 to 4 minutes total. Turn the fish over and grill, rotating it again halfway through, for 3 to 4 minutes.

4. Drizzle the arctic char with the pear butter sauce, and serve immediately.

4 servings

SALMON WITH SWEET CORN, TOMATO, AND AVOCADO RELISH

I've been making this dish for many years. With sweet corn and tomatoes in season at the same time, it makes for an incredible relish that suits just about any grilled fish—but I find it's particularly at home with salmon.

2 large ears fresh yellow corn, husked and silk removed

2 large Creole or other vine-ripened tomatoes, cored and cut into 3/4-inch dice (about 2 cups)

2 Hass avocados, peeled, pitted, and cut into 1/2-inch dice (about 2 cups)

6 tablespoons finely chopped red onion

2 tablespoons chopped fresh parsley

2 tablespoons extra-virgin olive oil

1 tablespoon freshly squeezed lemon juice

2 teaspoons salt

1/2 teaspoon freshly ground white pepper

Four 6-ounce pieces salmon fillet, skin on

1 tablespoon olive oil

1/2 teaspoon Emeril's Original Essence or Creole Seasoning (page 25)

1. Bring a large saucepan of water to a boil. Add the corn and simmer until tender, about 4 minutes. Drain. When it is cool enough to handle, cut the kernels from the ears and place them in a medium bowl.

2. Add the tomatoes, avocados, red onion, parsley, olive oil, lemon juice, 1 teaspoon of the salt, and 1/4 teaspoon of the white pepper to the corn. Toss to combine, and set aside.

3. Preheat the grill to medium-high.

4. Lightly brush the fish with the olive oil, and season it evenly with the Original Essence, the remaining 1 teaspoon salt, and the remaining 1/4 teaspoon white pepper. Place the fish on the grill, skin side down, and cook until the skin is crisp, 4 to 5 minutes. Turn, and cook until the salmon is opaque and medium-rare, about 4 minutes, depending upon the thickness of the fillet.

5. Serve the salmon with the relish spooned over the top.

4 servings

SAMBAL SHRIMP

If you are looking for a simple, impressive, flavor-packed, beautiful dish to serve a crowd, don't go any farther. This is it! It will blow your mind. My mouth is watering, just thinking about it.

. . . .

2 cups sambal oelek
(ground fresh chili paste)

1/2 cup sugar

1/2 cup freshly squeezed lime juice

1/2 cup olive oil

1/4 cup minced garlic

1/4 cup minced fresh ginger

1/4 cup mirin

2 tablespoons Vietnamese
fish sauce (nuoc nam)

2 tablespoons dark Asian
sesame oil

3 pounds large shrimp (about 30
shrimp), peeled and deveined,
head and tail segments intact

2 tablespoons roughly chopped
fresh cilantro

2 tablespoons roughly chopped
fresh mint

1. In a medium bowl, combine all the ingredients except the shrimp, cilantro, and mint. Whisk well to combine. Allow the marinade to sit at room temperature for at least 1 hour and up to 4 hours.

2. Place the shrimp in a 1-gallon resealable plastic bag, and add all but 1/2 cup of the marinade to the bag. Allow the shrimp to marinate at room temperature for 1 hour.

3. Preheat a grill to medium-high and oil the grill.

4. Place the shrimp on the grill and cook until they are just cooked through, 2 to 2 1/2 minutes per side. Transfer the cooked shrimp to a large bowl. Add the reserved 1/2 cup marinade, the cilantro, and the mint, and toss well to combine. Transfer the shrimp to a large serving bowl or platter, and serve immediately.

6 to 8 servings

YELLOWFIN TUNA WITH GRILLED PINEAPPLE SALSA

This dish exemplifies simplicity at its best.

. . . .

1 pineapple, peeled and cut into
 $^{1}/_{2}$-inch-thick rounds
 (see page 238)

6 tablespoons olive oil

$^{1}/_{4}$ cup finely chopped red onion

$^{1}/_{4}$ cup minced red bell pepper

$^{1}/_{4}$ cup rice vinegar

2 jalapeños, seeded and minced

2 tablespoons freshly squeezed
 lime juice

1 tablespoon finely chopped
 fresh cilantro

1$^{1}/_{2}$ teaspoons minced garlic

1$^{1}/_{2}$ teaspoons salt

Four 6-ounce yellowfin tuna steaks

1 tablespoon Emeril's Original
 Essence or Creole Seasoning
 (page 25)

Fresh cilantro sprigs, for garnish

1. Preheat a grill or grill pan to medium-high.

2. Brush both sides of the pineapple slices with 1 tablespoon of the olive oil. Place the pineapple on the grill and cook, rotating the slices occasionally, until slightly softened and nicely marked by the grill, 2 to 3 minutes per side. Remove from the grill and allow to cool to room temperature.

3. Dice the pineapple slices (discard the tough core portions), and place the dice in a medium nonreactive bowl. Add the red onion, bell pepper, rice vinegar, jalapeños, lime juice, cilantro, and minced garlic. Drizzle with 3 tablespoons of the remaining olive oil, and stir well to combine. Season with $^{1}/_{2}$ teaspoon of the salt, and set the salsa aside.

4. Season the tuna steaks with the remaining 1 teaspoon salt and the Original Essence, and brush with the remaining 2 tablespoons olive oil. Place the steaks on the grill, rotating them 45 degrees after 2 minutes. Cook for 2 minutes longer. Turn to the other side, grilling the steaks for an additional 2 minutes, or until medium-rare. Remove the tuna from the heat and let it rest briefly before serving it with the Grilled Pineapple Salsa. Garnish with cilantro sprigs.

4 servings

BACON-WRAPPED DIVER SCALLOPS WITH SOY GLAZE AND CHIVES

Talk about a childhood memory! Bacon-wrapped anything is a hit in my book, but the soy glaze adds a whole other dimension. Make sure you use super-fresh large sea scallops and good-quality bacon for this dish.

½ cup soy sauce

2 tablespoons sugar

12 long strips thinly sliced bacon

12 large diver scallops
  (10 per pound)

1 teaspoon salt

1 teaspoon freshly ground
  white pepper

6 metal skewers

1 tablespoon finely sliced chives

1. Preheat the oven to 350°F.

2. Combine the soy sauce and sugar in a 2-quart saucepan, and bring to a boil. Then lower the heat to a simmer and cook until the mixture has reduced to a glaze-like consistency, about 10 minutes. Set the soy glaze aside to cool.

3. Preheat a grill to medium. Line a rimmed baking sheet with aluminum foil.

4. Arrange the bacon slices in one even layer on the prepared baking sheet, and place it in the oven. Cook until the bacon begins to render its fat and change color, about 10 minutes. Remove from the oven and set aside until cool enough to handle.

5. Season the scallops with the salt and white pepper. Wrap each scallop with one of the cooled bacon strips, setting it seam side down to prevent the bacon from unrolling. Once all of the scallops are wrapped, place 2 scallops side by side with the seam sides touching. Use a metal skewer to pierce the scallops from side to side so that the skewer passes through the bacon and the scallops. Repeat with the remaining scallops and skewers. Turn the skewered scallops in the bacon fat remaining in the baking sheet. Set aside.

6. Spray or brush the grill grate with vegetable oil, and lay the scallops on the grill (be sure to have a spray bottle handy so you can spray the grill with water to reduce flare-ups). Cook for 2½ minutes. Then rotate the scallops 90 degrees and cook for an additional 2½ minutes. Turn the scallops over and cook for 2 to 4 minutes, or until they are just cooked through and the bacon is caramelized around the edges.

7. Remove the scallops from the grill, place them on a sheet pan, and brush the soy glaze over both sides. Serve on a platter, and garnish with the shaved chives.

6 appetizer servings

FISH "ON THE HALF SHELL"

Want to talk about letting the good times roll? This is a traditional way of grilling drum in the South, but if you can't find this type of fish in your area, substitute any fresh-caught fish with large scales, such as striped bass. Cooking it this way, with the scales still on, keeps the fish extra-moist and prevents it from sticking to the grill grate. Once cooked, the fish is easily removed from the skin before serving.

2 whole fish fillets, skin and scales on, from one 4- to 5-pound black drum, puppy drum, or sheepshead, pinbones removed

Kosher or sea salt and freshly ground black pepper

¼ cup extra-virgin olive oil

4 tablespoons (½ stick) butter, melted

2 tablespoons minced fresh soft mixed herbs, such as thyme, chives, parsley, oregano

1 tablespoon Emeril's Original Essence or Creole Seasoning (page 25)

1 tablespoon minced garlic

1. Preheat a grill to medium.

2. Season the flesh side of the fish fillets with salt and pepper to taste.

3. In a small bowl, combine the olive oil, butter, herbs, Original Essence, and garlic. Mix well to combine. Using a small spoon or a basting brush, liberally coat the flesh side of both fillets with the oil-herb mixture. Place the fish fillets on the grill, scale side down, and close the grill. Cook for 3 minutes. Open the grill and brush the fillets again with the oil-herb mixture. Close the grill and cook for another 3 minutes. Repeat this process until the flesh is firm and opaque, for a total cooking time of 14 to 15 minutes for fish fillets this size. Remove from the grill and serve immediately.

4 to 6 servings

SEA BASS PEPERONATA

Traditionally, this Italian recipe is a mixture of sweet peppers, tomatoes, onions, and garlic cooked in olive oil. We made our own version with some other flavorful ingredients. Serve hot and feel your taste buds explode!

Four 6- to 8- ounce, 1- to 1½-inch-thick pieces of farm-raised Chilean sea bass fillet

4 tablespoons olive oil

1 tablespoon plus 1 teaspoon Emeril's Original Essence or Creole Seasoning (page 25)

1 teaspoon salt, plus more to taste

½ teaspoon freshly ground white pepper, plus more to taste

1 cup thinly sliced onion

½ cup thinly sliced red bell pepper

½ cup thinly sliced green bell pepper

½ cup thinly sliced yellow bell pepper

⅓ cup pitted black olives, such as Kalamata

1 tablespoon minced garlic

2 teaspoons minced anchovy fillets

1 tablespoon nonpareil drained capers

½ cup dry white wine

3 tablespoons butter, cut into pieces

2 tablespoons finely chopped fresh parsley

1 tablespoon chopped fresh basil

1 tablespoon chopped fresh oregano

1. Preheat a grill to medium-low.

2. Rub the fish fillets with 2 tablespoons of the olive oil, and season them on both sides with the Original Essence, salt, and white pepper. Place the fish on the grill and cook until the fillets are just cooked through and the flesh flakes easily, 5 to 6 minutes on each side, depending on the thickness of the fillet.

3. While the fish is cooking, heat the remaining 2 tablespoons olive oil in a sauté pan. Add the onions and sauté for 1½ minutes. Then add the bell peppers, olives, garlic, anchovies, and capers, and sauté for 2 minutes. Add the wine and bring to a boil. Reduce the heat and simmer for 2 minutes. Fold in the butter, 1 tablespoon at a time, to thicken. Stir in 1 tablespoon of the parsley, the basil, and the oregano. Remove from the heat and season with salt and white pepper to taste.

4. Spoon the sauce onto the center of an oblong platter. Lay the fish directly on top of the sauce, garnish with the remaining 1 tablespoon parsley, and serve.

4 servings

GRILLED CLAMS CASINO

Everyone knows how delicious Clams Casino can be, but have you had them on the grill? Oh, baby. You can always make the casino butter in advance—all you do is cook the bacon and then the rest is absolutely simple. Wait until you taste this.

. . . .

2 strips thickly sliced applewood-smoked bacon

4 ounces andouille sausage

1 cup finely diced onion

1 cup finely diced red bell pepper

2 tablespoons fine dry breadcrumbs

8 tablespoons (1 stick) unsalted butter, at room temperature

1 tablespoon plus 1 teaspoon freshly squeezed lemon juice

2 tablespoons minced garlic

1 tablespoon chopped fresh parsley

24 littleneck clams, scrubbed

1. Heat a large nonstick sauté pan over medium-low heat. Add the bacon and cook, turning the slices occasionally, until just crisp, about 20 minutes. Let cool, and then cut into a total of twenty-four ¾-inch pieces. Set the bacon pieces aside. Discard all but 2 tablespoons of the bacon drippings.

2. Place the andouille sausage in a food processor and pulse until finely chopped. Add 1 tablespoon of the reserved bacon drippings to the same sauté pan, and add the processed andouille. Cook until the sausage has rendered its fat and browned, about 12 minutes. Transfer the sausage to paper towels to drain.

3. Add the remaining 1 tablespoon bacon drippings to the pan and increase the heat to medium-high. Add the onion and red bell pepper and cook, stirring constantly, until soft, 7 to 8 minutes. Remove the vegetables from the pan and set them aside to cool.

4. In a clean food processor bowl, combine the breadcrumbs, butter, lemon juice, garlic, parsley, andouille sausage, and the cooled onions and bell pepper. Pulse until well combined. Transfer the butter mixture to a piece of parchment or waxed paper, and roll the paper around it to form a tight cylinder. Chill in the refrigerator until firm, at least 2 hours prior to cooking and up to 2 days in advance.

5. Preheat a grill to medium-high.

6. Place the clams on the grill and cook until the shells pop open, 1 to 2 minutes. Remove the clams from the grill, and when they are cool enough to handle, remove the top shells. Divide the butter mixture evenly among the clams. Top each clam with one piece of the bacon. Return the clams to the grill and cook until the butter has melted and the liquid is bubbling, 1 to 2 minutes. Serve immediately.

About 4 servings

WHOLE BRONZINI, MEDITERRANEAN-STYLE

Also known as Mediterranean sea bass, this fish has become quite popular in the past few years. The simple flavors here combine to really surprise you.

4 whole bronzini or other small Mediterranean fish (about 1 pound each), gutted and scaled with heads left on, rinsed and patted dry

24 fresh thyme sprigs

2 teaspoons coarse sea salt, plus more to taste

1 teaspoon freshly ground black pepper

³/₄ cup olive oil

2 lemons, cut into ¹/₃-inch-thick rounds

¹/₄ cup freshly squeezed lemon juice

¹/₄ cup extra-virgin olive oil

1 tablespoon chopped fresh thyme leaves

1. Preheat a very clean and very well-oiled grill to high.

2. Lay the fish alongside each other on a clean kitchen towel, and gently roll together into a cylinder to remove excess moisture. (It is very important that the fish is sufficiently dry.) Transfer the fish to a rimmed baking sheet. Stuff the cavity of each fish with 6 thyme sprigs, and season the insides with 1 teaspoon of the sea salt and ¹/₂ teaspoon of the black pepper. Pour ¹/₂ cup of the olive oil over the fish and turn them in the oil to generously coat both sides. Sprinkle both sides of the fish evenly with the remaining 1 teaspoon sea salt and ¹/₂ teaspoon black pepper.

3. Oil the grill grate one more time, and place the fish directly on the grill. Reduce the heat to medium and cook, undisturbed and turning only once, until the flesh flakes easily and is just cooked through, about 5 minutes per side. (If you try to turn the fish too soon, they will stick to the grill. Be patient here and the fish will turn easily once the skin has crisped.)

4. While the fish is cooking, place the lemon slices on the grill and brush them lightly with some of the remaining ¹/₄ cup olive oil. Cook until softened and nicely marked on both sides, 2 to 3 minutes per side.

5. Transfer the fish to a platter and drizzle them with the lemon juice and extra-virgin olive oil. Sprinkle with the thyme leaves and additional sea salt if desired. Garnish with the grilled lemon slices. Serve immediately.

4 servings

CHORIZO-FLAVORED CATFISH WITH GRILLED TOMATO SALSA

The first time I tasted this dish, the flavors of smoked paprika and garlic, which to me scream "chorizo," really brought me back to my roots in Fall River. Who would have thought these flavors would feel so at home with fresh Mississippi catfish? It's pure magic.

½ cup olive oil

2 tablespoons minced garlic

4 teaspoons sweet pimentón
(Spanish smoked paprika)

Six 6-ounce catfish fillets

1 tablespoon kosher salt

Grilled Tomato Salsa
(recipe follows)

1. Preheat a grill to medium, and oil the grate well. Line a rimmed baking sheet with aluminum foil.

2. In a small bowl, combine the olive oil, garlic, and pimentón, stirring well to combine. Place the catfish on the prepared baking sheet and spoon the olive oil mixture evenly over each fillet. Using your hands, massage the oil into the fillets, coating both sides. Allow the fish to sit for 20 minutes.

3. Season the fish with the kosher salt. Lay the fillets, bone side down, on the grill and cook for 1½ minutes. Rotate the fish 90 degrees and grill for an additional 1½ minutes. Then turn the fish over and cook just until it is cooked through, 2 to 2½ minutes. Remove the catfish from the grill and serve with the Grilled Tomato Salsa.

6 servings

Grilled Tomato Salsa

1½ pounds Roma tomatoes,
    halved
½ red onion, peeled
3 tablespoons olive oil
1½ teaspoons salt,
    plus more for seasoning before grilling
½ teaspoon freshly ground black pepper,
    plus more for seasoning before grilling
6 tablespoons extra-virgin olive oil
3 tablespoons roughly chopped
    fresh parsley
2 tablespoons nonpareil drained capers
Juice of 1 lemon
2 teaspoons minced garlic
1½ teaspoons sweet pimentón
    (Spanish smoked paprika)

1. Preheat a grill to medium, and oil the grate well.

2. In a large bowl, combine the tomatoes, onion half, and olive oil. Season lightly with salt and pepper, and toss well to combine. Lay the tomatoes on the grill, cut side down, and cook for 1½ minutes. Rotate them 90 degrees and cook for an additional 1½ minutes. Then turn the tomatoes over and cook for 2 minutes. Remove them from the grill and set aside.

3. Place the onion on the grill and cook for 3 minutes. Rotate it 90 degrees and cook for an additional 3 minutes. Then turn the onion over and cook for 2 to 4 minutes. Remove the onion from the grill and let it cool slightly.

4. Once they are cool enough to handle, roughly chop the grilled tomatoes and place them in a large bowl. Finely chop the grilled onion and add it to the bowl. Add the 1 1/2 teaspoons salt, ½ teaspoon pepper, extra-virgin olive oil, parsley, capers, lemon juice, garlic, and pimentón, and stir well to combine. Allow the salsa to sit for at least 1 hour at room temperature before serving.

Note: You can prepare the salsa a day in advance and store it in the refrigerator. Make sure to allow it to come to room temperature before serving.

About 3 cups

KICKED-UP FISH IN A BAG

Looking for clean flavors and a healthful, straightforward way to prepare fish? This is it—an updated papillote! Even though I've called for rainbow trout fillets here, feel free to use whatever fish is available and whatever vegetables you like. Just keep in mind that thick fillets will need a longer cook time. I try to use recycled aluminum foil if it's available; it's good to be "green."

Two or three 8-ounce zucchini, sliced into ¼-inch-thick rounds

1⅓ cups finely julienned carrots

Four 4-ounce rainbow trout fillets

2 teaspoons salt

1 teaspoon freshly ground white pepper

1 tablespoon plus 1 teaspoon minced garlic

¼ cup chopped fresh parsley

1 tablespoon plus 1 teaspoon chopped fresh basil

1 tablespoon plus 1 teaspoon chopped fresh mint

1 tablespoon plus 1 teaspoon chopped fresh cilantro

1 tablespoon plus 1 teaspoon chopped fresh chives

1 tablespoon plus 1 teaspoon chopped fresh tarragon

1 tablespoon plus 1 teaspoon finely grated Parmesan cheese

¼ cup pine nuts, lightly toasted

¼ cup white balsamic vinegar

¼ cup plus 1 tablespoon extra-virgin olive oil

1. Preheat a grill to low.

2. Cut 4 pieces of aluminum foil, each about 14 X 14 inches. In the center of each piece of foil, arrange 12 to 15 slices of zucchini overlapping, creating three columns and four or five rows. Place ⅓ cup of the julienned carrots on top of each portion of zucchini. Place 1 trout fillet on top of each mound of carrots, and season each with ½ teaspoon salt and ¼ teaspoon white pepper. Spread 1 teaspoon of the minced garlic over each fillet. Combine the herbs in a small bowl, mix well, and divide the mixture evenly among the 4 fillets. Top each fish with 1 teaspoon of the Parmesan and 1 tablespoon of the pine nuts. Combine the vinegar and the olive oil in a small bowl and whisk to mix well; divide the mixture evenly among the fillets. Bring the edges of the foil up so that they meet, then fold them together several times to seal the "bag" well on all sides.

3. Place the bags on the grill and cover the grill. Cook until the trout is cooked through and the vegetables are crisp-tender, 8 to 10 minutes. Remove the bags from the grill and carefully (watch out for steam!) open them. Serve the opened pouches in wide, shallow bowls.

4 servings

PROVENÇAL ROUGET

Red mullet, or *rouget*, as it is called in Europe, is not as popular here in the U.S. But oh, it's a delicious little fish. Prepared with herbes de Provence, this takes me back to when I was a young cook, just out of culinary school, lucky enough to have the opportunity to work for a while in the South of France.

Twelve 8-ounce whole rougets, cleaned, gutted, and scaled

1½ cups plus 2 tablespoons olive oil

1 tablespoon herbes de Provence, plus more for garnish

Salt and freshly ground black pepper, to taste

14 ounces baby eggplants, halved lengthwise

14 ounces large cherry tomatoes, halved lengthwise

1 tablespoon chopped fresh thyme

1 tablespoon chopped fresh basil

¾ cup freshly squeezed lemon juice

1 teaspoon sea salt, for garnish (optional)

1. Preheat a grill to medium-high.

2. Dry the fish thoroughly with paper towels. Place the fish in a baking dish or on a platter, and pour ¾ cup of the olive oil over them. Sprinkle them with the 1 tablespoon herbes de Provence, and season lightly with salt and pepper. Turn the fish to coat them all over. Set aside to marinate for 15 minutes while you prepare the vegetables.

3. Place the eggplant and tomato halves on another platter and drizzle with ¼ cup plus 2 tablespoons of the remaining olive oil. Season with salt and pepper, and toss to coat evenly. Grill the vegetables, cut side down, until nicely marked and softened: about 10 minutes total for the eggplant and 2 minutes total for the tomatoes. Set the vegetables aside on a platter and cover it loosely with foil to keep them warm.

4. Make sure the grill grates are very clean, and oil them very well. Grill the fish until they are just cooked through and the flesh flakes easily, 4 to 6 minutes per side. Just before removing the fish from the grill, sprinkle the thyme and basil over them, and drizzle with the remaining 1/2 cup olive oil, the lemon juice, and a final sprinkling of herbes de Provence. Arrange the fish on the platter with the grilled vegetables, and garnish with the sea salt if desired.

6 to 8 servings

Things
WITH
WINGS

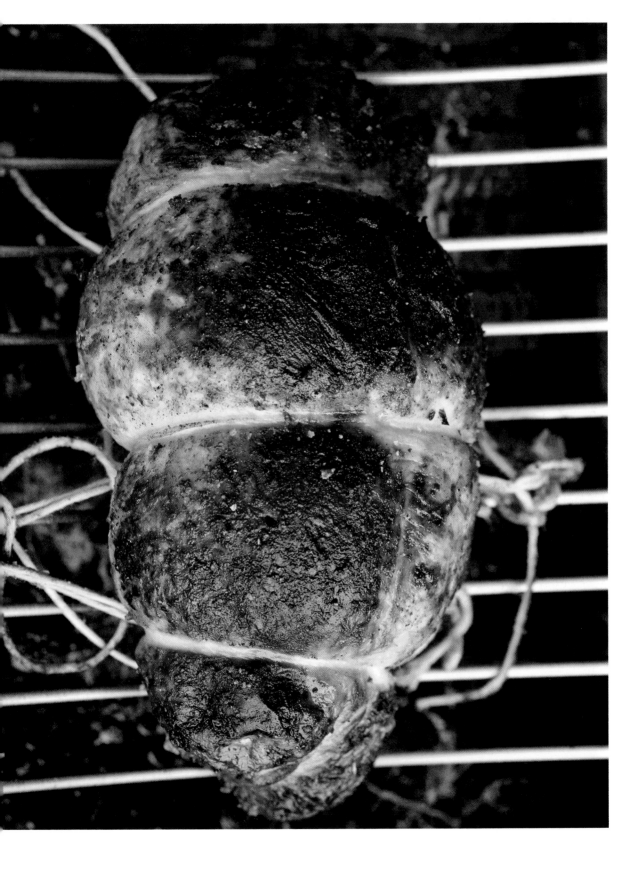

BACON-WRAPPED QUAIL WITH BOURBON-PEPPER JELLY GLAZE

This is a little tribute to my dear friend Fireman Paul. Boy, can he cook!

$\frac{1}{2}$ cup red pepper jelly

3 tablespoons bourbon

$\frac{1}{2}$ teaspoon Worcestershire sauce

8 quail (about 5$\frac{1}{2}$ ounces each), dressed

1 teaspoon salt

1 teaspoon freshly ground black pepper

8 strips thickly sliced bacon

1. Preheat a grill to medium-low.

2. In a small bowl, whisk the pepper jelly, bourbon, and Worcestershire together until smooth. Set the glaze aside.

3. Season each quail with $\frac{1}{8}$ teaspoon of the salt and $\frac{1}{8}$ teaspoon of the pepper. Wrap a bacon strip around each quail and secure it with a toothpick.

4. Place the bacon-wrapped quail on the grill and cook, turning them frequently, until the bacon is beginning to caramelize in places and the quail have grill marks on all sides, 10 to 12 minutes. Brush the quail with the glaze and continue turning, glazing, and cooking until the birds are nicely glazed and grilled on all sides and the flesh is just cooked through, about 10 minutes longer. Let the quail rest briefly before serving.

4 servings (2 quail per person)

VIETNAMESE-STYLE CHICKEN WINGS

This dish is inspired by the talents of my culinary assistant, Alain Joseph—and let me tell you, these wings are so delicious, they're gonna knock your socks off!

3 to 3½ pounds chicken wings, separated at the joints, tips reserved for another use

½ cup roughly chopped lemongrass bases

¼ cup chopped shallots

¼ cup chopped fresh ginger

3 tablespoons chopped green onions (white part only)

3 tablespoons packed light brown sugar

2 tablespoons roughly chopped garlic

⅓ cup Vietnamese fish sauce (nuoc nam)

3 tablespoons freshly squeezed lime juice

3 tablespoons peanut oil

1 teaspoon salt

¼ cup chopped dry-roasted salted peanuts

¼ cup chopped fresh cilantro

1. Rinse the wing pieces under cold running water and pat them dry with paper towels. Set them aside in a resealable plastic bag.

2. Combine the lemongrass, shallots, ginger, green onions, brown sugar, garlic, fish sauce, lime juice, and peanut oil in a food processor and process until smooth. Pour the marinade over the chicken wings, and seal the bag. Refrigerate overnight.

3. Preheat a grill to medium.

4. Remove the chicken wings from the marinade, reserving the marinade. Place the wings on the grill and season them with the salt. Cook, turning frequently and basting often with the marinade, for 15 minutes. Discard any remaining marinade and continue to grill the wings until cooked through, 8 to 10 minutes longer.

5. Place the chicken on a platter, and garnish with the chopped peanuts and cilantro. Serve immediately.

4 to 6 appetizer servings

CILANTRO-TEQUILA GRILLED CHICKEN

This marinade also works great for flank steak and grilled fish. Hey, what doesn't taste good with a little cilantro, tequila, and lime?

½ cup tightly packed fresh cilantro leaves

5 cloves garlic, peeled

1 shallot, roughly chopped

½ serrano chile, seeded and chopped

1 tablespoon cumin seeds, toasted

¼ cup freshly squeezed lime juice

¼ cup olive oil

¼ cup tequila

1 teaspoon salt, plus more for seasoning before grilling

½ teaspoon freshly ground black pepper, plus more for seasoning before grilling

4 chicken leg quarters (or 8 pieces bone-in, skin-on chicken thighs and legs)

Fresh cilantro sprigs, for garnish

Lime wedges, for garnish

1. Combine all the ingredients except the chicken, cilantro sprigs, and lime wedges in a blender or food processor, and puree until smooth, stopping to scrape down the sides of the bowl as needed. Place the chicken pieces in a baking dish or in a resealable plastic bag, and pour the marinade over the chicken. Marinate, refrigerated, for at least 2 hours and up to 4 hours, turning the bag occasionally.

2. Preheat a grill to medium.

3. Remove the chicken from the marinade and discard the marinade. Pat the chicken dry with paper towels, and lightly season the pieces with salt and pepper on both sides. Place the chicken on the grill and cook for 8 to 10 minutes. Turn the chicken over and cook for an additional 8 to 10 minutes. Continue cooking the chicken, turning it as needed to promote even browning, until it is cooked through and tender, 25 to 30 minutes total for separate thighs and drumsticks and 35 to 40 minutes for whole chicken legs. (An instant-read thermometer inserted into the thickest part of the chicken should register 165°F.)

4. Remove the chicken from the grill and let it rest for 5 minutes before serving. Garnish the chicken with cilantro sprigs and lime wedges.

6 to 8 servings

FILIPINO-INSPIRED ADOBO CHICKEN THIGHS

This version of adobo chicken brings all the wonderful flavors of the classic dish right on home. You and your family will keep coming back for more! Try serving it with buttered white rice and a simple salad.

1¼ cups plus 1 tablespoon cider vinegar

½ cup plus 1 tablespoon soy sauce

¼ cup minced garlic

2 bay leaves

8 bone-in, skin-on chicken thighs

¼ cup honey

Olive oil, for brushing

1 teaspoon salt

½ teaspoon freshly ground black pepper

1. Combine ¼ cup of the vinegar, 3 tablespoons of the soy sauce, garlic, and bay leaves in a resealable plastic bag. Add the chicken thighs and turn to coat them evenly. Seal the bag and marinate the chicken for at least 4 hours in the refrigerator.

2. Preheat a grill to medium.

3. Combine 1 cup of the remaining vinegar, the remaining ¼ cup plus 2 tablespoons soy sauce, and the honey in a 1-quart saucepan. Bring to a boil and immediately turn down to a simmer. Continue to cook until the mixture thickens enough to coat the back of a spoon and is reduced by half, 11 to 13 minutes. Stir in the remaining 1 tablespoon vinegar. Remove from the heat and set aside to cool.

4. Remove the chicken from the bag (discard the marinade), and pat it dry with paper towels. Brush the chicken with olive oil and season it with the salt and pepper. Place the chicken on the grill and cook, turning frequently, until it is just cooked through and a thermometer inserted into the thickest part of the thigh (without touching the bone) registers 165°F, 20 to 25 minutes. Transfer the chicken to a platter, drizzle the vinegar-soy sauce over it, and serve.

About 4 servings

BACKYARD BARBECUED CHICKEN WITH HOMEMADE BBQ SAUCE

This kid-friendly dish is about as simple as it gets, my friends. If you don't have the time to prepare the homemade barbecue sauce, simply make sure to buy a quality bottled sauce.

. . . .

8 whole chicken leg quarters

Salt and freshly ground black pepper, to taste

2 cups Homemade BBQ Sauce (recipe follows)

1. Preheat a grill to medium-low, and brush the grate with oil.

2. Season both sides of the chicken legs with salt and pepper. Place the chicken on the grill, skin side down, and cook, adjusting the chicken's position and turning the pieces occasionally, until it appears to be about halfway cooked, about 15 minutes. Then use a basting brush to brush the chicken legs with the barbecue sauce, and continue to cook, turning the pieces frequently and reapplying barbecue sauce each time the chicken is turned, until it is cooked through and an instant-read thermometer inserted into the thickest part registers 160° to 165°F, 15 to 20 minutes. Serve the chicken hot or warm.

6 to 8 servings

Homemade BBQ Sauce

2 tablespoons vegetable oil
3/4 cup chopped yellow onion
2 tablespoons chopped garlic
4 cups ketchup
1/2 cup packed dark brown sugar
2 tablespoons cane syrup
1/2 cup cider vinegar
1/4 cup Worcestershire sauce
3 tablespoons red hot sauce
2 tablespoons yellow mustard

2 teaspoons Emeril's Original Essence or Creole
 Seasoning (page 25)
1/2 teaspoon crushed red pepper, or more to taste

Heat the oil in a large pot over medium-high
heat. Add the onion and cook, stirring, for 4
minutes. Add the garlic and cook, stirring, for 1
minute. Add all the remaining ingredients, and
bring to a boil. Lower the heat to a simmer and
cook, stirring occasionally, until the sauce has
thickened and the flavors have married, 15 to 20
minutes. Remove from the heat and set aside to
cool.

Note: Any unused sauce can be stored in an airtight nonreactive container in the refrigerator for
up to 2 weeks. **About 4 cups**

GRILLED CHICKEN THIGHS WITH BRAZILIAN "VINAIGRETTE" SALSA

Chicken thighs are an incredibly flavorful yet inexpensive cut of chicken. Because they have just the right amount of fat, they always come out terrifically moist and juicy. The Brazilian-style salsa here can be made a couple of hours ahead of time and kept at room temperature until you are ready to serve it.

8 skin-on, boneless chicken thighs

2 teaspoons coarse sea salt

6 tablespoons ($3/4$ stick) butter, melted

2 tablespoons minced garlic

1 teaspoon ground bay leaf

Brazilian "Vinaigrette" Salsa (recipe follows), for serving

1. Preheat a grill to medium-low.

2. Season the chicken with the sea salt.

3. In a small bowl, combine the butter, garlic, and bay leaf.

4. Place the chicken, skin side down, on the grill and brush it with the butter-garlic blend. Cook for 7 minutes. Turn the chicken over, baste it with more of the butter mixture, and cook for another 7 minutes. Turn the chicken skin side down, and cook for 7 minutes more. Turn it over one last time and cook until an instant-read thermometer inserted into the deepest portion of the thighs registers 160° to 165°F, about 7 minutes longer. Remove from the pan, and serve with the "Vinaigrette" Salsa.

4 to 6 servings

Brazilian "Vinaigrette" Salsa

1 cup peeled, seeded, and diced tomato (¼-inch dice)
½ cup diced red bell pepper (¼-inch dice)
½ cup diced green bell pepper (¼-inch dice)
3 tablespoons white wine vinegar
3 to 4 tablespoons olive oil
Salt and freshly ground black pepper, to taste

Combine all the ingredients in a medium bowl and stir well to combine. Allow the salsa to sit at room temperature for at least 1 hour before serving.

2 cups

GRILLED CHICKEN BREASTS WITH SPICY GREEN MOLE

This is a take on one of Mexico's traditional dishes. The sauce is a blend of herbs, spices, pepitas, tomatillos, and poblanos—a delicious and complex combination. The sauce is best made just before cooking the chicken. If you make the sauce far in advance, it is likely that you will need to thin it with a small amount of broth or water when reheating it.

1 tablespoon tamarind paste

³/₄ cup plus 1 tablespoon vegetable oil

1¹/₂ teaspoons chopped garlic

¹/₂ cup chopped onion

¹/₄ cup plus 2 tablespoons chopped fresh cilantro

1 teaspoon Emeril's Southwest Essence spice blend, plus more for seasoning before grilling

4 boneless, skinless chicken breast halves (about 2 pounds)

4 tomatillos, husks removed, rinsed under hot water

¹/₂ cup hulled raw pumpkin seeds (pepitas)

¹/₂ teaspoon ground coriander

¹/₂ teaspoon ground cumin

1 clove garlic, peeled

2 poblano chiles (about 3 ounces), roasted, peeled, and chopped

1 cup roughly chopped romaine lettuce leaves

¹/₂ teaspoon kosher salt, plus more for seasoning

1¹/₂ cups chicken broth, plus more if needed (see headnote)

1. In a small bowl, whisk together the tamarind paste, ¹/₂ cup of the vegetable oil, the chopped garlic, ¹/₄ cup of the chopped onion, the 2 tablespoons chopped cilantro, and the 1 teaspoon Southwest Essence.

2. Place the chicken breasts in a gallon-size resealable plastic bag, pour the tamarind marinade into the bag, and seal it. Refrigerate for at least 2 hours and up to overnight.

3. To make the mole, heat a medium sauté pan over medium heat. Add the tomatillos and dry-roast in the pan for 5 minutes, browning them on all sides. Remove the tomatillos and set them aside to cool. Then cut them into quarters.

4. Reduce the heat under the pan to low, and add the pumpkin seeds, coriander, and cumin. Toast the pumpkin seeds and spices in the pan for 3 minutes, stirring often. Transfer the seeds and spices to the bowl of a food processor.

5. Add the clove of garlic and the remaining ¼ cup chopped onion to the processor, and process for 1 minute, scraping down the sides of the bowl after 30 seconds. While the machine is running, add the tomatillos and roasted poblanos, and process for another minute, scraping down the sides of the bowl after 30 seconds. Add the romaine lettuce and process for 1 minute more.

6. Heat a medium saucepan over low heat and add the 1 tablespoon vegetable oil. Once it is hot, add the mole and cook for 5 minutes. Season with the ½ teaspoon kosher salt, and add the 1½ cups chicken broth. Simmer the mole, stirring it occasionally, until thickened, 30 minutes. Remove the pan from the heat and stir in the ¼ cup chopped cilantro. Set aside and keep warm until ready to serve the chicken.

7. Preheat a grill to medium-low.

8. Remove the chicken breasts from the marinade. Brush them with the remaining ¼ cup vegetable oil, and season them liberally with Southwest Essence. Sprinkle with kosher salt. Lay the chicken breasts on the grill and cook for 3 minutes. Rotate the chicken breasts 90 degrees to make grill cross marks, and cook for another 3 minutes. Then turn the chicken over and repeat, cooking until the chicken is nicely browned and the internal temperature registers 165°F on an instant-read thermometer, about 12 minutes total.

9. Serve the chicken immediately, with the warm mole sauce spooned generously over the top.

Note: The tamarind in the marinade can burn easily; make sure to turn the chicken more frequently if necessary.

4 servings

NORTHERN ITALIAN-STYLE CHICKEN UNDER A BRICK

What a concept. What a dish! Any old bricks will do for this purpose—just make sure that they are well wrapped in foil, preferably recycled foil if available. The weight of the bricks holds the chicken down firmly and helps to create a crisp crust while the chicken cooks.

1 cup olive oil

1/2 cup freshly squeezed
    lemon juice

2 tablespoons minced garlic

1 tablespoon grated lemon zest

1 tablespoon chopped
    fresh rosemary

1 tablespoon chopped fresh thyme

1 tablespoon chopped fresh parsley

1 teaspoon kosher salt

1/2 teaspoon crushed red pepper

One 3- to 3 1/2-pound chicken

2 bricks, completely wrapped in
    aluminum foil

2 teaspoons Emeril's Original
    Essence or Creole Seasoning
    (page 25)

1/2 teaspoon salt

1/2 teaspoon freshly ground
    white pepper

1. In a small mixing bowl, combine the olive oil, lemon juice, garlic, lemon zest, rosemary, thyme, parsley, kosher salt, and crushed red pepper. Mix to combine, and set the marinade aside.

2. Place the chicken on a cutting board. With a boning knife and/or poultry scissors, cut along both sides of the backbone and remove it. Place the chicken skin side down, and using a paring or small boning knife, cut underneath and around the breastbone on both sides, cutting the cartilage away from the flesh so that you can work your fingers underneath the bone, and then carefully remove the breastbone. The chicken should now lie flat like an open book. Tuck the wing tips behind the wing joint that meets the breast. Cut small slits in the skin that hangs beneath the thighs, and tuck the tips of the drumstick bones inside. Place the chicken in a 13 X 9-inch nonreactive baking dish, and pour the marinade over it. Refrigerate, covered, for at least 2 hours and up to 6 hours, turning the chicken occasionally in the marinade.

3. Preheat the oven to 500°F, and preheat a grill to medium-low.

4. Heat the bricks in the oven for 20 minutes. (Alternatively, heat the bricks on the grill for 30 minutes.)

5. Remove the chicken from the marinade (discard the marinade), and season it on both sides with the Original Essence, salt, and white pepper.

6. Place the chicken, skin side down, on the grill, and set the bricks on top of the chicken to cover it completely and flatten it. Cook until the skin has nice grill marks, about 15 minutes. Then turn the chicken 45 degrees and cook until a second set of grill marks forms, creating a crosshatch pattern, about 15 minutes longer.

7. Using pot holders or thick kitchen towels, remove the bricks and set them aside. Carefully turn the chicken over so that it is now skin side up. Cook until the juices run clear and an instant-read thermometer inserted into the deepest portion of the thigh registers 165°F, about 15 minutes. Remove the chicken from the grill, place it on a cutting board, and let it rest for 5 minutes. Then cut the chicken into quarters and serve immediately.

Note: The cooking time may vary slightly, depending on your grill.

4 servings

ASIAN SPICY BARBECUED CHICKEN

I just love the Asian flavors used in this chicken dish. Simple and fantastic.

1 tablespoon dark Asian sesame oil

1 tablespoon peanut oil

1/2 cup minced onion

1 teaspoon minced garlic

1 teaspoon minced fresh ginger

1/4 cinnamon stick (about 1 inch)

1/2 whole star anise

1/4 cup freshly squeezed lime juice

2 tablespoons soy sauce

1/2 cup plum sauce

1/2 teaspoon crushed red pepper

1/4 cup water

1 teaspoon dry mustard

2 teaspoons kosher salt

1/2 teaspoon Chinese five-spice powder

One 3 1/2- to 4-pound chicken, cut into 8 pieces

1. Place a small saucepan over medium-high heat, and add the sesame and peanut oils. Once the oil is hot, add the onion and cook, stirring often, until soft and slightly translucent, 3 to 4 minutes. Add the garlic, ginger, cinnamon stick, and star anise, and cook for 30 seconds. Add the lime juice and soy sauce, and deglaze the pan. Cook until the liquid has reduced by half. Add the plum sauce, crushed red pepper, water, and mustard. Reduce the heat to a simmer and cook for 5 minutes. Remove the sauce, and discard the cinnamon stick and star anise. Set aside.

2. Combine the kosher salt and five-spice powder in a small bowl and stir to mix well. Season the chicken with the mixture, and set it aside for 20 minutes.

3. Preheat the oven to 400°F, and preheat a grill to medium. Line a rimmed baking sheet with aluminum foil.

4. Place the chicken pieces on the grill and cook for 4 minutes. Rotate them 45 degrees, and cook for 4 minutes longer. Turn the chicken over and cook for 4 minutes. Then rotate it 45 degrees and cook for a final 5 minutes. Transfer the chicken to the prepared baking sheet, brush it with the barbecue sauce, and place the baking sheet in the oven. Cook until the chicken is just cooked through and an instant-read thermometer inserted into the deepest part of the thigh, without touching a bone, registers 165°F, about 10 minutes. Remove the chicken from the oven and let it rest for a few minutes before serving.

4 to 6 servings

CHICKEN PAILLARDS OVER ARUGULA

Paillard is a fancy word that simply means something flattened. Chicken paillards are often breaded and fried, but here we simply season the chicken, quickly grill it, and serve it over lightly dressed arugula. Talk about flavors that really pop! The trick is not to overcook the chicken so that it stays wonderfully tender and juicy.

Four 6- to 8-ounce boneless,
skinless chicken breast halves

5 ounces fresh arugula or baby
greens, tough stems removed,
rinsed and spun dry

3 tablespoons plus 2 teaspoons
extra-virgin olive oil,
plus more for serving

2 1/2 teaspoons freshly squeezed
lemon juice, plus more for
serving

1 3/4 teaspoons salt

Freshly ground black pepper

Emeril's Original Essence or
Creole Seasoning (page 25)

1/4 cup coarsely grated
Parmigiano-Reggiano cheese

1. Preheat a grill to high, and lightly coat the grate with oil.

2. Place each chicken breast half between two sheets of plastic wrap. With the flat side of a meat mallet or the side of a cleaver, working from the center of the meat outward, gently pound it to a thickness of 1/4 inch. Refrigerate, still between the plastic wrap, for at least 5 minutes.

3. In a large bowl, combine the arugula, 1 tablespoon of the olive oil, 1 teaspoon of the lemon juice, 1/4 teaspoon of the salt, and a pinch of black pepper. Toss gently to combine. Adjust the seasoning to taste, and divide the greens among four large plates.

4. In a small bowl, combine the remaining 2 tablespoons plus 2 teaspoons olive oil with the remaining 1 1/2 teaspoons lemon juice, 1/2 teaspoon of the salt, and a pinch of black pepper. Stir to blend.

5. Remove the top piece of plastic wrap from each chicken breast. Rub about 3/4 teaspoon of the olive oil mixture over the exposed side and season it lightly with Original Essence. Season each chicken breast on both sides with 1/4 teaspoon of the remaining salt.

6. Carefully place the chicken, oiled side down, on the hot grill and quickly peel away the remaining piece of plastic wrap. Using a spoon, dab the remaining olive oil mixture onto the exposed chicken and rub it evenly over the meat. Cook until the chicken is firm to the touch and just cooked through, 1 to 2 minutes per side.

7. To serve, place 1 chicken breast in the center of each arugula salad, and drizzle each one lightly with additional extra-virgin olive oil and fresh lemon juice. Sprinkle 1 tablespoon of the grated Parmesan on top of each serving, and serve immediately.

4 servings

TURKEY ROULADE WITH PEACH AND SAGE GRAVY

There is something very special about a roulade—and it's not as hard as it looks. If you're in the mood for something different during the holiday season and feel like cooking outdoors, you just may want to try this. Just keep in mind that the trick is to properly flatten the turkey breast before you stuff, roll, and tie it.

4 quarts water

1 cup packed light or
   dark brown sugar

³⁄₄ cup kosher salt, plus more
   in seasoning the roulade

One 7-pound whole turkey breast,
   skin on, deboned (see Note)

4 cups coarse fresh breadcrumbs
   (from a loaf of French or
   Italian bread)

8 ounces bacon, chopped and
   cooked until crisp, fat reserved
   (or substitute olive oil)

2 tablespoons unsalted butter,
   melted

2 tablespoons chopped garlic

¹⁄₂ cup chopped fresh parsley

1 teaspoon Emeril's Original
   Essence or Creole Seasoning
   (page 25), plus more for
   seasoning before grilling

¹⁄₄ cup olive oil

Freshly ground black pepper

Peach and Sage Gravy
   (recipe follows)

1. Combine the water, brown sugar, and kosher salt in a 2-gallon or larger stockpot or other nonreactive container, and whisk until the sugar and salt have dissolved. Place the turkey breast in the stockpot and refrigerate for 8 hours.

2. Remove the turkey breast from the brine, and pat it dry with paper towels. (At this point you can proceed with the recipe or refrigerate the turkey up to 1 day until ready to cook.)

3. Preheat a grill to low.

4. Cut three lengths of kitchen twine to 32 inches, and lay them across a cutting board. Making sure the skin is pulled down to cover as much of the breast meat as possible, lay the turkey breast, skin side down, on top of the strings. Cover the turkey with parchment paper or plastic wrap, and pound it with a heavy mallet or the bottom of a cast-iron skillet until the thickest part of the breast is no more than 2 inches thick.

5. In a large mixing bowl, use a rubber spatula to combine the breadcrumbs, bacon, ¼ cup reserved bacon fat, butter, garlic, parsley, and Original Essence.

6. Lightly season the turkey breast with Original Essence. Pack the stuffing mixture tightly into a 1-cup measure, and then empty the stuffing onto the middle of the breast. Repeat this two more times. Roll the breast up as tightly as you can to form a cylinder, and use the twine to tie the breast together in three places. Snip off any extra length of twine. (You can also tie a piece of twine vertically around the breast, tucking in the flaps at the end, if you find this is necessary to keep the stuffing inside.) Brush the olive oil all over the roulade, and season it lightly with Original Essence, kosher salt, and pepper.

7. Place the turkey roulade, seam side up, onto the coolest part of the grill. Close the grill cover and cook for 30 minutes. Rotate the roulade 90 degrees and cook for another 15 minutes. Then turn the roulade over and cook, uncovered, for 15 minutes, or until the internal temperature reaches 160°F when tested with an instant-read thermometer. Remove the turkey from the grill and let it rest for 10 minutes before carving.

8. Remove the strings and slice the roulade crosswise into ½-inch-thick slices. Serve with the Peach and Sage Gravy.

Note: If you do not feel comfortable deboning a skin-on turkey breast, kindly ask a butcher to do it for you.

6 to 8 servings

Peach and Sage Gravy

This simple gravy is made with peach preserves, so you can enjoy it even when peaches are not in season, making this a year-round dish.

2 tablespoons olive oil
1/4 cup finely minced shallots
2 teaspoons minced garlic
1/2 cup white wine vinegar
4 cups turkey stock, chicken stock,
    or canned low-sodium chicken broth
3/4 cup peach preserves
2 tablespoons unsalted butter, at room temperature
2 tablespoons all-purpose flour
1 1/4 teaspoons salt
3/4 teaspoon freshly ground black pepper
1/3 cup fresh sage leaves

1. Set a 2-quart saucepan over medium heat and add the olive oil. Once the oil is hot, add the shallots and garlic and sauté, stirring often, until the shallots are fragrant and lightly caramelized, about 1 minute. Add the white wine vinegar and cook until it is nearly completely reduced, about 1 minute. Add the stock and preserves, and raise the heat to high.

2. While the stock is coming to a boil, combine the butter and flour in a small bowl, and using the back of a spoon, blend to form a smooth paste.

3. Add the butter-flour paste to the stock, and use a whisk to stir it in, making sure that it is well incorporated. Bring the gravy to a boil, season it with the salt and pepper, and reduce the heat to a simmer. Cook until the gravy has reduced by one quarter, about 20 minutes.

4. Remove the pan from the heat and add the sage leaves to the gravy. Allow the flavors to steep for about 3 minutes, and then strain the gravy. Serve the gravy with slices of the turkey roulade.

About 3 cups

"BEER CAN" TURKEY BREAST WITH BBQ GRAVY

This dish is a spin on the popular "beer can chicken" that many folks cook in their barbecue pits. Well, I've worked with my partners at All-Clad, and we have come up with a very cool cast-iron vertical roaster. You pour liquid into the inner well and set the bird on top, and it is continuously moistened while cooking. Every morsel will be incredibly juicy. The great thing is that it can go in the oven or on the grill and works well with either chicken or turkey. You can make a sauce from the fabulous juices—it's awesome!

4 quarts water

1 cup packed light or dark brown sugar

³/₄ cup kosher salt, plus more for seasoning the turkey

One 7-pound turkey breast, skin on, rib bones and backbone intact

2 cups chopped onions (¹/₂-inch pieces)

1 cup chopped celery (¹/₂-inch pieces)

8 garlic cloves, peeled and smashed

10 sprigs fresh oregano, tied into a bundle with kitchen twine

3 teaspoons Emeril's Rib Rub spice blend

¹/₄ cup plus 2 tablespoons olive oil

2 cups canned chopped tomatoes, with their juice

Emerilware Cast Iron Vertical Poultry Roaster

1¹/₄ cups beer (one 12-ounce bottle)

Freshly ground black pepper, to taste

Chicken broth, as needed

¹/₂ cup cider vinegar

¹/₄ cup packed dark brown sugar

2 tablespoons molasses

¹/₂ teaspoon salt

¹/₂ teaspoon dried oregano

¹/₂ teaspoon crushed red pepper

1. Combine the water, brown sugar, and ¾ cup kosher salt in a 2-gallon or larger stockpot or other nonreactive container, and whisk until the sugar and salt have dissolved. Submerge the turkey breast in the brine and refrigerate it for 8 hours.

2. Remove the turkey from the brine, rinse it, and pat it dry with paper towels. Refrigerate, covered, until ready to cook.

3. Preheat a grill to medium-high.

4. In a medium bowl, combine the onions, celery, garlic, oregano bundle, 1 teaspoon of the Rib Rub, and the 2 tablespoons olive oil. Add 1 cup of the tomatoes, and stir together. Pour the vegetables into the outer well of the vertical roaster. Fill the inner well with beer, and pour the remaining beer over the vegetables.

5. Brush the remaining ¼ cup olive oil over the turkey breast. Sprinkle the remaining 2 teaspoons Rib Rub over the outside of the turkey, and season it lightly with kosher salt and black pepper.

6. Position the turkey breast over the inner well of the roaster so that it sits securely upright. Place the roaster on the grill, close the lid, and cook, basting every 20 minutes with the accumulated pan juices, until the turkey is golden brown and an instant-read thermometer inserted into the deepest portion of the breast registers 165°F, usually about 1 hour. (If the skin browns too quickly during cooking, cover the turkey with foil. If the liquid in the well of the roaster evaporates during cooking and before the turkey is done, add more chicken broth as necessary.)

7. Remove the roaster from the grill, and set the turkey on a cutting board to rest for 10 minutes before carving. Transfer the vegetables and pan juices from the inner and outer wells of the roaster to a blender, and set aside.

8. While the turkey is resting, make the gravy: In a small saucepan, whisk together the vinegar, remaining 1 cup canned tomatoes, dark brown sugar, molasses, salt, oregano, and crushed red pepper. Bring to a boil. Then reduce the heat to a simmer and cook until the flavors blend and the sauce thickens slightly, about 15 minutes.

9. Add the barbecue sauce to the vegetables in the blender, and blend until smooth. (Please be cautious while blending the hot sauce, as the steam may cause the top of the blender to open. Either hold the lid down with a towel or wait for the sauce to cool slightly before blending.) Transfer the gravy to a bowl or sauceboat, and keep it warm until ready to serve.

10. Carve the turkey breast into thin slices, and serve with the BBQ gravy.

6 to 8 servings

EMERIL'S "JERK" CHICKEN WITH GINGERED BBQ DRIZZLE

True Jamaican jerk chicken is an experience you're likely not to forget—it's a mixture of so many different aromatic spices, it's just incredible. Try our simplified version here. The Scotch bonnet is one of the most intensely spicy chile peppers in the world, so feel free to cut back on the number of chiles if you're not a fan of intense heat. Do take the time to make the Gingered BBQ Drizzle. Though it's not authentically Jamaican, and though this chicken is super-flavorful on its own, the drizzle is icing on the cake. And, hey, the marinade and sauce both work well with pork tenderloins, too, in case you want to change it up a bit.

12 to 14 green onions, white part only, chopped (about ³⁄₄ cup)

8 Scotch bonnet or habanero chiles, stems and seeds removed

¹⁄₃ cup minced garlic

¹⁄₃ cup minced fresh ginger

¹⁄₄ cup freshly squeezed lime juice

3 tablespoons dark rum

3 tablespoons soy sauce

2 tablespoons light brown sugar

1 tablespoon fresh thyme leaves

2 tablespoons pumpkin pie spice

1 fryer chicken, cut into 8 pieces

Vegetable oil, for brushing

1 tablespoon kosher salt

Gingered BBQ Drizzle (recipe follows), for serving

1. Combine the green onions, chiles, garlic, ginger, lime juice, rum, soy sauce, brown sugar, thyme, and pumpkin pie spice in a food processor, and process to form a smooth paste.

2. Place the chicken in a gallon-size resealable plastic bag, add the marinade, and seal. Refrigerate, turning the bag occasionally, for at least 4 hours and up to 24 hours.

3. Heat a grill to medium-low, and lightly oil the grate.

4. Remove the chicken from the marinade (discard the marinade). Wipe the chicken with paper towels to remove any excess marinade. Brush the chicken with vegetable oil, and season it on both sides with the kosher salt. Place the chicken, skin side down, on the grill and cook, turning and rotating frequently, until it is lightly charred and just cooked through and an instant-read thermometer inserted in the thickest part (avoiding the bone) registers 165°F, 30 to 35 minutes. Remove the chicken from the grill and let it rest for 5 minutes before serving.

5. Serve with the Gingered BBQ Drizzle.

About 4 servings

Gingered BBQ Drizzle

6 tablespoons ketchup
1/4 cup firmly packed dark brown sugar
1/4 cup pineapple juice
2 tablespoons distilled white vinegar
2 tablespoons freshly squeezed lime juice
2 tablespoons minced fresh ginger
1 tablespoon butter
1 tablespoon dry mustard
1 tablespoon minced garlic
1 tablespoon salt
1 tablespoon tamarind paste, such as Tamicon
1 tablespoon Worcestershire sauce
1/2 Scotch bonnet chile, seeded and minced

Combine all the ingredients in a small saucepan and cook over medium heat until reduced enough to coat the back of a spoon, about 10 minutes. Serve the sauce warm or at room temperature, drizzled over the jerk chicken. **About 1 cup**

TANDOORI-STYLE CHICKEN DRUMSTICKS

I decided to take this popular Indian dish and interpret it on the grill—and it came out great. Traditionally, this would be cooked in a clay oven called a *tandoor*. We just kept the exotic flavors by using a marinade made with creamy, tangy yogurt, bright spices, and aromatic vegetables. Just the right punch. Just the right spice.

12 chicken drumsticks
(about 3½ pounds)

2 tablespoons vegetable oil,
plus extra for brushing

½ cup chopped white onion

2 tablespoons plus 1 teaspoon
chopped garlic

2 tablespoons plus 1½ teaspoons
chopped fresh ginger

1 teaspoon finely chopped serrano
or jalapeño chile

1 tablespoon sweet paprika

2¼ teaspoons salt

1 teaspoon ground cumin

1 teaspoon ground turmeric

1 teaspoon ground coriander

1 teaspoon garam masala

½ teaspoon cayenne pepper

1½ cups plain whole-fat yogurt

2½ tablespoons freshly squeezed
lemon juice

½ teaspoon kosher salt

¾ teaspoon freshly ground
white pepper

¼ cup chopped mint

1 tablespoon honey

1. Place the chicken in a baking dish.

2. Combine the oil, onion, the 2 tablespoons garlic, the 2 tablespoons ginger, and the serrano pepper in a blender, and process on high speed until it forms a smooth paste. Add the paprika, 1½ teaspoons of the salt, and the cumin, turmeric, coriander, garam masala, and cayenne, and continue to process until well blended. Add ½ cup of the yogurt and 1 tablespoon of the lemon juice, and process again to form a smooth sauce, scraping down the sides of the bowl as necessary. Pour the marinade over the chicken and turn to coat the pieces evenly. Cover the baking dish tightly with plastic wrap, and refrigerate for at least 4 hours and up to 24 hours, turning the chicken occasionally.

3. Preheat a grill to medium.

4. Remove the chicken from the marinade and pat it dry with paper towels. Brush the chicken with vegetable oil, and season it with the kosher salt and ¼ teaspoon of the white pepper. Place the chicken on the grill and cook for 10 to 12 minutes on the first side, turning and rotating as necessary. Cook on the second side for 10 to 12 minutes, or until the chicken is just cooked through and an instant-read thermometer inserted into the thickest part of the drumstick (without touching the bone) registers 160° to 165°F. Remove the chicken from the grill and let it rest briefly.

5. While the chicken is resting, make the yogurt dipping sauce by combining the remaining 1 cup yogurt, the mint, the honey, remaining 1 teaspoon garlic, remaining 1½ teaspoons ginger, remaining 1½ tablespoons lemon juice, remaining ¾ teaspoon salt, and remaining ½ teaspoon white pepper in a food processor and pulsing until well incorporated. Transfer to a serving bowl and serve with the chicken.

4 servings

OFF THE
Land

NEW YORK STRIP WITH STILTON-WALNUT BUTTER

Man, talk about a classic combination. I just love Stilton—it's one of the top three blue cheeses in the world. It's especially nice when mixed with walnuts and sitting on top of a good old New York strip steak. Oh, baby.

Four 10-ounce New York strip steaks

1 cup port wine

8 tablespoons (1 stick) unsalted butter, at room temperature

4 ounces Stilton cheese, crumbled (about 1 cup), at room temperature

$1/4$ cup chopped toasted walnuts

2 tablespoons kosher or coarse sea salt

1 tablespoon freshly ground coarse black pepper

1. Place the steaks in a resealable plastic bag or a shallow container, and drizzle the port over them. Seal the bag or cover the container, and refrigerate for 2 to 3 hours, turning the steaks occasionally.

2. In a small bowl, stir together the butter and Stilton until creamy. Stir in the walnuts. Using a rubber spatula, transfer the butter to a piece of waxed paper. Wrap the paper around it, forming a log. Refrigerate until firm, about 2 hours.

3. Preheat a grill to high, and oil the grate well.

4. Remove the steaks from the marinade (discard the marinade) and pat them dry. Season both sides of the steaks with the salt and pepper. Place the steaks on the hot grill and cook for 4 to 5 minutes on each side for medium-rare, or to the desired degree of doneness. Remove the steaks from the grill and let them rest for 5 minutes before serving. Serve topped with generous tablespoonfuls of the walnut-Stilton butter.

Note: The walnut-Stilton butter can be kept in the refrigerator for several days or in the freezer for up to 2 months.

4 servings

LAMB T-BONES WITH A RED WINE REDUCTION SAUCE

Oh, these little babies are so fantastic! The T-bone is without a doubt one of my favorite cuts of lamb. If you don't see these at your local market, don't be shy—make friends with the butcher! Try serving these with the Grilled Smashed Potatoes on page 20.

2 teaspoons olive oil

2 teaspoons minced shallots

$\frac{1}{4}$ teaspoon minced garlic

$\frac{3}{4}$ cup dry red wine

2 teaspoons chopped fresh rosemary

$1\frac{1}{2}$ cups lamb or veal stock

$1\frac{1}{4}$ teaspoons salt

$\frac{3}{4}$ teaspoon freshly cracked black pepper

8 lamb T-bones

8 tablespoons (about 4 ounces) Irish Cashel Blue cheese or your favorite blue cheese

4 sprigs fresh rosemary, for garnish (optional)

1. Place a 1-quart saucepan over medium-high heat, and add the olive oil. Once the oil is hot, add the shallots and sauté for 1 minute. Add the garlic and sauté for 30 seconds. Add the red wine and deglaze the pan. Add the chopped rosemary, and cook until the wine has nearly evaporated, 4 to 5 minutes. Add the lamb stock, and season with $\frac{1}{4}$ teaspoon of the salt and $\frac{1}{4}$ teaspoon of the pepper. Bring the sauce to a boil. Then reduce the heat to a gentle boil and cook until the sauce is reduced to about 1 cup, about 10 minutes. Set the sauce aside and keep it warm while you prepare the lamb.

2. Preheat a grill to medium, and lightly coat the grate with oil.

3. Season the lamb T-bones on both sides with the remaining 1 teaspoon salt and $\frac{1}{2}$ teaspoon black pepper. Place the lamb on the grill and cook for 2 minutes. Rotate the lamb 45 degrees and cook for an additional 2 minutes. Then turn the lamb over and cook for a final 2 minutes.

4. To serve the lamb, place 2 T-bones in the center of each dinner plate and drizzle them with the red wine reduction sauce and crumbles of blue cheese. Garnish each plate with a rosemary sprig, if desired.

4 servings

THAI-STYLE BEEF SALAD

This dish is inspired by the Thai classic but has been adapted for the grill and the American home cook. My friend Angela, whose heritage is part Thai, turned us onto this in the test kitchen. Talk about good and simple!

One 1¾-pound flank steak

Emeril's Original Essence or Creole Seasoning, to taste (page 25)

¼ cup olive oil

1 tablespoon Worcestershire sauce

2 tablespoons jasmine rice

¼ cup Vietnamese fish sauce (nuoc nam), or to taste

¼ cup plus 2 tablespoons freshly squeezed lime juice, or to taste

¼ cup thinly sliced green onion tops

¼ cup thinly sliced shallots

¼ cup chopped fresh cilantro

¼ cup chopped fresh mint

2 teaspoons sugar

1 teaspoon crushed red pepper

4 cups thinly sliced napa cabbage

2 cups thinly sliced red cabbage

1 cucumber, halved lengthwise and thinly sliced on the diagonal, for garnish

1. Season the flank steak with Original Essence on both sides. Place the steak in a gallon-size resealable plastic bag, add the olive oil and Worcestershire, and seal the bag. Marinate in the refrigerator for at least 4 hours and up to overnight.

2. Preheat a grill or broiler to medium-high.

3. Place the jasmine rice in a small skillet and heat it over medium-high heat, stirring constantly, until it is toasted, golden brown, and fragrant, 6 to 7 minutes. Transfer the rice to a plate and let it cool. When the rice has cooled, place it in a clean coffee grinder or spice mill, and process it to a fine powder. Set the rice powder aside.

4. Remove the steak from the marinade (discard the marinade). Grill the steak for 3 to 4 minutes on each side for medium-rare. Remove it from the grill and let it rest for 10 minutes.

5. Thinly slice the steak against the grain, reserving any accumulated juices.

6. Place the fish sauce, lime juice, reserved steak juices, green onions, shallots, cilantro, mint, ground jasmine rice, sugar, and crushed red pepper in a bowl, and whisk to combine.

7. In another mixing bowl, combine the cabbages with 3 tablespoons of the dressing. Toss well, and arrange on a platter. Toss the steak with the remaining dressing, and arrange the steak slices and dressing over the top of the cabbage. Serve immediately, garnished with the cucumber slices.

About 4 servings

BUFFALO RIB-EYES WITH A BLUE CHEESE GLAÇAGE

If you can't find buffalo steaks at your local grocery store, try ordering them off the Internet or from a specialty butcher shop. The intense flavor is really worth the effort, and the lean meat is also naturally lower in calories than regular beef steaks.

4 ounces blue cheese, crumbled

1/4 cup buttermilk

1/4 cup panko breadcrumbs

2 tablespoons chopped pecans

1 tablespoon chopped fresh thyme

1 tablespoon chopped fresh parsley

Salt and freshly ground black pepper

4 buffalo rib-eye steaks

1. Prepare the blue cheese glaçage by combining the blue cheese, buttermilk, breadcrumbs, pecans, thyme, and parsley in a bowl. Stir until well combined. Season to taste with salt and pepper, and set aside.

2. Preheat a grill to medium-high.

3. Season the steaks on both sides with salt and pepper to taste. Place them on the grill and cook for 4 to 6 minutes on one side. Turn the steaks over, and place several tablespoons of the blue cheese glaçage on top of each steak. Cook for 4 to 6 minutes for medium-rare. Remove the steaks from the grill and let them rest for a couple of minutes before serving.

4 servings

ITALIAN-STYLE GRILLED T-BONE STEAKS

This is one of the most popular dishes served at several of my restaurants. For all you T-bone fans out there, this one's for you.

3 T-bone steaks, about 1½ inches thick and 1½ to 2 pounds each, at room temperature

½ cup plus 1 tablespoon extra-virgin olive oil

2 tablespoons kosher salt

1 tablespoon freshly cracked black pepper

6 ounces fresh arugula, rinsed and spun dry

2 tablespoons freshly squeezed lemon juice, or more to taste

1½ teaspoons coarse sea salt, or more to taste

½ cup 1-inch-wide strips of shaved Parmigiano-Reggiano cheese, for garnish

1. Preheat a grill to medium-high.

2. Rub each steak with 1 tablespoon of the olive oil, and season each steak with 2 teaspoons of the kosher salt and 1 teaspoon of the cracked black pepper.

3. Grill the steaks, rotating them 90 degrees midway through cooking, for 6 to 8 minutes. Turn the steaks over and grill, rotating them midway through cooking, for 6 to 8 minutes for medium-rare. Transfer the steaks to a platter and let them rest for 5 minutes before serving.

4. When you are ready to serve them, slice the two sides of each steak away from the T-shaped bone, and then very thinly slice each portion of steak against the grain. Divide the arugula evenly among six large dinner plates, and arrange the steak slices evenly on top of the greens. Drizzle any accumulated meat juices over the meat. Sprinkle 1 teaspoon of the lemon juice and 1 tablespoon of the remaining olive oil over each plate. Sprinkle ¼ teaspoon of the sea salt over each plate, and serve immediately, garnished with the strips of Parmigiano-Reggiano.

6 servings

EJ'S SIMPLE OVEN-BBQ RIBS

This is truly one of the first dishes that brought a connection between my son, EJ, and myself a few years back. The great thing, other than its being very simple, is that if you find yourself facing inclement weather when you're planning to grill, this recipe can still make everyone happy. You can finish the ribs on the grill if you like, or you can schmear 'em up with barbecue sauce and finish them in the oven. The secret to the success of this dish is the long, slow cooking time.

2 racks baby back ribs

6 tablespoons Emeril's Rib Rub spice blend

1½ teaspoons salt

1 teaspoon freshly ground black pepper

1 teaspoon celery salt

Emeril's Sweet Original Bam BQ Barbecue Sauce, or your favorite barbecue sauce

1. Preheat the oven to 300°F. Line a large baking sheet with a piece of aluminum foil that is large enough to cover the pan twice (you will be folding this over the ribs and sealing it).

2. Arrange the ribs, meat side up, in one layer on the prepared baking sheet. In a small bowl, combine the Rib Rub, salt, pepper, and celery salt, and stir to combine. Divide the seasoning evenly between the 2 slabs of ribs, coating them well on both sides. Fold the extra length of foil over the ribs, and seal it tightly on all sides. Place the baking sheet in the oven and bake, undisturbed, for 2½ to 3 hours, or until the ribs are very tender.

3. Preheat a grill to medium-high (or leave the oven on).

4. Remove the baking sheet from the oven and peel back the foil so that the ribs are exposed. Using a basting brush or the back of a spoon, coat the meaty side of the rubs lightly with barbecue sauce. Place the slabs of ribs, meaty side up, on the grill and cook until the barbecue sauce is thickened and lightly browned, 5 to 10 minutes. (Alternatively, return the baking sheet to the oven and continue to bake the ribs, without the foil covering, until the barbecue sauce is thickened and lightly browned, 20 to 30 minutes.)

5. Remove the ribs from the grill (or oven), and let them cool briefly. Then cut between the ribs and serve, with additional barbecue sauce on the side if desired.

2 to 4 servings

PIRI-PIRI CARNE SPART

When I was a little boy, I would attend weekend Portuguese festivals where you could go to a booth and buy these strips of steak that were threaded onto a long metal rod. You'd pay the man, season the meat, and grill it over an open flame. Then you would add some piri piri (Portuguese hot sauce with flavor and power) and wrap it all up in crusty Portuguese bread. Delicious!

1½ cups olive oil

4 jalapeños, stemmed, seeded, and finely chopped

2 poblano chiles, stemmed, seeded, and finely chopped

1 tablespoon crushed red pepper

1 teaspoon salt

1 teaspoon freshly ground black pepper

1 tablespoon minced garlic

1 tablespoon finely chopped fresh cilantro, plus more for garnish

1 tablespoon kosher salt

2 pounds boneless beef steak, sirloin cut into ½-inch-thick slices

Metal skewers or long bamboo skewers (soak bamboo skewers in warm water for at least 1 hour)

Emeril's Original Essence or Creole Seasoning, for garnish (page 25)

1. Combine the olive oil, jalapeños, chiles, crushed red pepper, salt, and black pepper in a saucepan, and bring to a boil. Reduce the heat to a simmer and cook for 4 minutes. Remove the pan from the heat and stir in the garlic. Using an immersion blender, puree the sauce until smooth. (Alternatively, allow the mixture to cool slightly, then transfer it to a regular blender and puree until smooth.) Stir in the cilantro and kosher salt. Transfer the sauce to a nonreactive container and refrigerate it for up to 1 week.

2. Place the meat in a nonreactive bowl, add 1 cup of the piri piri sauce, and toss to combine. Then transfer the bowl, covered, to the refrigerator and allow the meat to marinate for at least 4 hours and up to overnight.

3. Preheat a grill to medium-high.

4. Remove the beef from the marinade, and thread the strips onto the skewers. Place the skewers on the grill, and cook for 2 to 3 minutes on each side.

5. Meanwhile, place the remaining piri piri in a saucepan and bring it to a simmer.

6. Place the skewers on a platter, and drizzle with the piri piri. Garnish with chopped cilantro and Original Essence, and serve.

4 servings

BRINED BABY BACK RIBS WITH A SPICY APPLE GLAZE

The key to succulent, juicy ribs done on the grill is long, slow cooking, so this is one recipe you shouldn't consider if you're in a hurry. But, boy, the reward is worth it. The Spicy Apple Glaze is delicious and also works well with grilled pork.

4 quarts cold water

1 cup kosher salt

1/2 cup packed light brown sugar

2 slabs baby back ribs
(3 1/2 to 4 pounds)

4 teaspoons Smoky Paprika Rub
(page 207)

Spicy Apple Glaze
(recipe follows)

1. Place the water, kosher salt, and brown sugar in a large stockpot, and stir well to dissolve the salt and sugar. Submerge the baby back ribs in the mixture and refrigerate for 1 1/2 hours.

2. Remove the ribs from the brine (discard the brine), and pat them dry with paper towels. Season on both sides with the Smoky Paprika Rub and let sit at room temperature for 30 minutes.

3. While the ribs are resting, preheat a grill to medium-low.

4. If using a gas grill, turn off the power to one side of the grill and lay the ribs, meat side down, on the cool end of the grill. If using a charcoal grill, load the charcoal to one side of the grill and place the ribs on the cool side of the grill, meat side down. Close the lid and cook the ribs for 1 hour, rotating the racks back to front and side to side midway through cooking.

5. Turn the ribs over so that they are now meat side up. Continue cooking the ribs until they are very tender, about 3 hours longer, rotating the racks back to front and side to side every 30 minutes. During the last 30 minutes of cooking, brush the ribs with 1/2 cup of the Spicy Apple Glaze.

6. Remove the ribs from the grill, cut between the bones, and serve the ribs, drizzled with the remaining Spicy Apple Glaze.

4 servings

Spicy Apple Glaze

3 cups apple cider
1 cup cider vinegar
1 cup applesauce
1 cup granulated sugar
$1/2$ cup packed light brown sugar
$1/4$ cup thinly sliced fresh ginger
$1/2$ cinnamon stick (about $1^1/2$ inches)
$1/2$ vanilla bean, split,
    seeds scraped out and reserved
6 cardamom pods
2 teaspoons minced garlic
2 teaspoons allspice berries
$1^1/2$ teaspoons crushed red pepper
$1/2$ teaspoon dry mustard
$1/4$ teaspoon salt

To make the glaze, combine all the ingredients, including the vanilla bean and seeds, in a 6-quart saucepan and bring to a boil over medium-high heat, stirring often to dissolve the sugar. Once the mixture has come to a boil, reduce the heat to medium and cook until it is reduced to a glaze consistency, 30 to 35 minutes. Remove the pan from the heat, and strain the glaze through a fine-mesh sieve into a bowl. Discard the solids. Set the glaze aside until ready to use. **About 1 cup**

CARIBBEAN PORK TENDERLOINS

One bite of this will transport you to soft, sandy beaches with turquoise blue waters and steel drums playing in the background! Serve these delicious tenderloins alone, or top them with the Grilled Pineapple Salsa on page 124.

½ small Vidalia onion, sliced

¼ cup minced fresh ginger

2 tablespoons minced garlic

2 Scotch bonnet chiles, stemmed, seeded, and minced

One 14-ounce can unsweetened coconut milk

½ cup dark rum

¼ cup freshly squeezed lime juice

3 tablespoons cane or dark brown sugar

Two 1- to 1½-pound pork tenderloins, trimmed of fat

Vegetable oil, for brushing

1 teaspoon kosher salt

½ teaspoon freshly ground black pepper

1 teaspoon chopped fresh cilantro

1. Combine the onion, ginger, garlic, chiles, coconut milk, rum, lime juice, and brown sugar in a bowl, and whisk to combine. Place the tenderloins in a gallon-size resealable plastic bag, and add the marinade. Remove as much air as possible before sealing the bag, and turn the bag to make sure the tenderloins are well coated. Refrigerate, turning the bag occasionally, for 6 hours.

2. Preheat a grill to medium-low.

3. Remove the tenderloins from the marinade (discard the marinade), and blot them dry with paper towels. Brush the tenderloins with vegetable oil, and season them with the salt and pepper. Place them on the grill and cook, rotating as necessary, until an instant-read thermometer inserted into the center of the tenderloins reads 140° to 145°F, 20 to 25 minutes. Remove them from the grill and let them rest for 10 minutes before slicing and serving. Garnish with the chopped cilantro.

About 4 servings

GRILLED MARINATED FLANK STEAK WITH CHIMICHURRI SAUCE

Chimichurri sauce is an Argentinean specialty that is particularly at home next to grilled meats. If you've not yet tried it, I bet you'll fall in love with its intense, full flavor. The only thing that could make this combo any better would be to serve it alongside the Avocado, Tomato, and Red Onion Salad on page 24.

1¹/₂ cups dry sherry

¹/₂ cup sherry vinegar

1 cup thinly sliced red onion

2 tablespoons minced garlic

¹/₂ cup olive oil

One 1¹/₂- to 2-pound flank steak

2 teaspoons salt

1 teaspoon freshly cracked
   black pepper

Chimichurri Sauce (recipe follows),
   for serving

1. In a shallow nonreactive bowl that is large enough to hold the steak, combine the sherry, sherry vinegar, red onion, garlic, and olive oil. Stir to blend well. Lay the steak over the marinade and turn so that it is coated on both sides. Wrap the bowl loosely in plastic wrap and refrigerate overnight, turning the steak occasionally.

2. Preheat a grill to high.

3. Remove the steak from the marinade (discard the marinade), and season it with the salt and pepper. Grill the steak for 4 to 5 minutes per side for medium-rare. Remove it from the grill and let it rest for 5 minutes. Then thinly slice the steak across the grain, and serve it with the Chimichurri Sauce.

4 to 6 servings

Chimichurri Sauce

1 cup extra-virgin olive oil
²/₃ cup sherry vinegar
2 tablespoons freshly squeezed lemon juice
1 cup chopped fresh flat-leaf parsley
¹/₄ cup chopped fresh basil
3 tablespoons minced garlic

2 tablespoons minced shallots
1 tablespoon chopped fresh oregano
½ teaspoon kosher salt
¼ teaspoon freshly cracked black pepper
¼ teaspoon crushed red pepper

Combine the olive oil, vinegar, lemon juice, parsley, basil, garlic, shallots, and oregano in a food processor, and pulse until well blended (do not puree). Stir in the kosher salt, black pepper, and crushed red pepper. Transfer the sauce to a nonreactive bowl, cover it with plastic wrap, and set it aside for at least 2 hours and up to 6 hours at room temperature. (The sauce will keep in an airtight nonreactive container in the refrigerator for up to 3 days.) **About 2½ cups**

EMERIL'S DELMONICO BONE-IN RIB STEAKS

This simple steak is one of our best-selling items on the menu at Delmonico Steakhouse, my restaurant in the Venetian Hotel in Las Vegas. It's all about the quality of the meat, so find a good butcher who specializes in prime aged beef and treat yourself to an intense, serious steakhouse experience at home.

Four 22- to 24-ounce bone-in rib steaks, preferably quality prime beef that has been wet and dry aged

2 tablespoons vegetable oil

Emeril's Original Essence or Creole Seasoning (page 25)

Kosher salt and freshly ground black pepper

1. Allow the steaks to come to room temperature for up to 1 hour.

2. Rub the steaks on both sides with the vegetable oil, and season them liberally with Original Essence, kosher salt, and pepper.

3. Preheat the oven to 450°F, and preheat a grill, grill pan, or cast-iron skillet to medium-high.

4. Grill the steaks until they are seared on both sides, about 4 minutes per side. Then transfer the steaks to a baking sheet, place it in the oven, and cook until the meat reaches the desired temperature, 140°F for medium-rare. Remove the steaks from the oven and let them sit for 5 minutes before slicing and serving.

4 manly servings

BALSAMIC-MARINATED RIB-EYES WITH BALSAMIC BARBECUE SAUCE

The Balsamic Barbecue Sauce elevates this simple rib-eye to something extraordinary. Make the sauce up to two weeks ahead of time—it keeps well in the refrigerator and tastes great in any preparation where you would consider using traditional barbecue or steak sauce.

1 cup balsamic vinegar

½ cup extra-virgin olive oil

2 tablespoons minced garlic

2 teaspoons crushed red pepper

Four 12- to 14-ounce rib-eye steaks

2 tablespoons Emeril's Original Essence or Creole Seasoning (page 25)

1 teaspoon kosher salt

Balsamic Barbecue Sauce (recipe follows), for serving

1. Place the balsamic vinegar, olive oil, garlic, and crushed red pepper in a 1-gallon resealable plastic bag. Add the steaks and seal the bag. Allow to marinate at room temperature for up to 2 hours.

2. Preheat a grill to medium.

3. Remove the steaks from the marinade (discard the marinade), and season them on both sides with the Original Essence and kosher salt. Place the steaks on the grill and cook for 6 minutes, rotating them 90 degrees after 3 minutes to make a crosshatch pattern. Turn the steaks over, brush them with 3 tablespoons of the barbecue sauce, and cook for 5 to 6 minutes for medium-rare. Remove the steaks from the grill and serve them immediately, with additional Balsamic Barbecue Sauce if desired.

4 servings

Balsamic Barbecue Sauce

2 tablespoons olive oil
¾ cup diced red onion (small dice)
1 tablespoon sliced garlic
1 cup balsamic vinegar
2 teaspoons light brown sugar
½ cup dry red wine, preferably Sangiovese
One 14.5-ounce can diced tomatoes,
    with their juices
1 tablespoon tomato paste
2 teaspoons liquid smoke
1 sprig fresh rosemary
Salt and freshly ground black pepper, to taste

Set a 1-quart saucepan over medium heat and add the olive oil. Add the red onion and garlic and sauté until the onions are lightly caramelized, 5 to 7 minutes. Add the balsamic vinegar and brown sugar, and bring to a boil. Cook until the vinegar is nearly completely reduced, about 10 minutes. Add the red wine and cook until reduced by half, about 5 minutes. Add all the remaining ingredients and cook until the sauce is slightly thickened, 7 to 8 minutes. Remove the pan from the heat, discard the rosemary sprig, and puree the sauce using an immersion blender. (Alternatively, set the sauce aside to cool briefly; then puree it in a standard blender.) Use immediately, or store in an airtight nonreactive container in the refrigerator for up to 2 weeks. **About 1¾ cups**

BIG PORTERHOUSE TUSCAN-STYLE, WITH HERBED GARLIC OLIVE OIL

The porterhouse cut is for the true steak aficionado, since you get a little bit of sirloin as well as some of the filet mignon all in one. Though the sizable steak called for here will likely be on the expensive side, keep in mind that this indulgent cut can serve quite a few folks! Low heat and slow cooking is the way to go with this one.

One 5½-pound porterhouse steak, in one piece, with ½ inch fat remaining on the fatty side

1 cup extra-virgin olive oil

Kosher salt and freshly ground black pepper

1½ teaspoons minced fresh oregano

1½ teaspoons minced fresh rosemary

4 cloves garlic, minced

1. Preheat a grill to low.

2. Rub the meat on all sides with ¼ cup of the olive oil, and season it liberally on all sides with kosher salt and black pepper. Place the meat on the grill, fatty side down first, and cook, turning it occasionally, until the meat is nicely browned on all sides and an instant-read thermometer inserted into the center registers 120°F, 1 hour and 20 minutes—and maybe longer, depending on your grill. Remove the steak from the grill and set it aside to rest for at least 15 minutes before serving.

3. In a small bowl, combine the remaining ¾ cup olive oil with the oregano, rosemary, and garlic, and season with kosher salt and black pepper to taste.

4. When ready to serve, cut the meat away from the bone so that it is in 2 large pieces. Thinly slice the pieces, and serve the slices, drizzled with the herbed garlic olive oil, making sure that each guest gets some of both the sirloin and the tenderloin.

4 to 6 servings

KOREAN-STYLE GRILLED SHORT RIBS

You know, I love short ribs—braised, oven-roasted, you name it! But there is something really special about finishing them on the grill when they're pre-pared with Korean flavors. Keep in mind that you'll need to purchase at least 1 pound of short ribs per person—and don't plan on having any leftovers!

4 pounds short ribs, cut into
   2-inch square pieces

1 cup orange juice

1 cup tamari

1/2 cup packed light brown sugar

1/4 cup honey

1 tablespoon minced garlic

1 tablespoon minced fresh ginger

1 tablespoon minced green onions,
   white and green parts

1 tablespoon hot pepper sesame oil

1 teaspoon crushed red pepper

1. Using a sharp knife, score the meaty side of each piece of short rib, making three perpendicular cuts halfway through the meat. (This will allow the mari-nade to penetrate the meat best.) Combine all of the remaining ingredients in a mixing bowl, and stir well. Place the short ribs in a 2-gallon resealable plastic bag, and pour the marinade over them. Seal the bag and marinate in the refrigerator overnight.

2. Preheat a grill to medium-high.

3. Remove the short ribs from the refrigerator and let them come to room temperature.

4. Remove the ribs from the marinade (discard the marinade), and place them on the grill, bone side down. Cook until well seared, 4 to 5 minutes. Reduce the heat to medium-low and cook the ribs, turning them frequently, until nicely browned on all sides, 14 to 16 minutes longer, or until at the desired degree of doneness. Remove the ribs from the grill and serve immediately.

4 servings

ORANGE, CUMIN, AND CILANTRO GRILLED PORK LOIN

I just love the flavors of orange and cumin with pork. The method here is a little different than you might expect—the loin is grilled briefly to seal in the juices, then transferred to a grill-proof pan and cooked with citrus juices. Oh, talk about moist! The pan juices make for a simple but intensely flavored "jus" for serving with the pork. Add a sweet potato dish to your menu, such as the Grilled Sweet Potato Salad on page 33, and you'll be set to feed a small crowd.

One 3½-pound boneless
   pork loin

2 tablespoons olive oil

1 tablespoon kosher salt

1½ teaspoons ground cumin

1½ teaspoons freshly ground
   black pepper

½ cup freshly squeezed orange
   juice

¼ cup freshly squeezed lime juice

¼ cup white wine vinegar

2 tablespoons orange marmalade

2 tablespoons chopped
   fresh cilantro

1. Preheat a grill to medium.

2. Rub the pork loin well on all sides with the olive oil, and season it with the kosher salt, cumin, and black pepper. Place the pork loin, fat side down, onto the grill and cook for 5 minutes. Rotate the pork 90 degrees and cook for another 5 minutes. Then turn the pork over and cook for a final 5 minutes. Remove the pork from the grill and place it in a small grill-proof roasting pan that holds it snugly.

3. In a medium bowl, combine the orange juice, lime juice, vinegar, and marmalade, and whisk well to combine. Drizzle the citrus mixture over the pork. Place the roasting pan directly on the grill, close the lid of the grill, and cook for 5 minutes. Raise the lid and baste the pork with the pan juices. Close the lid and cook for an additional 15 to 20 minutes, basting every 5 minutes, until the pork reaches an internal temperature of 140°F. (Take care not to overcook it.)

4. Remove the pork from the grill. Add the cilantro to the roasting pan, and swirl it in the pan juices. Allow the pork to rest for 7 to 10 minutes before slicing. Serve the pork thinly sliced, drizzled with pan juices.

6 to 8 servings

PORK CHOP PIPÉRADE

This flavorful dish is simple to put together. It is based on the classic pipérade, with its origins in the Basque region of France. The thing I love about this method is that it works well with fish and steak, too. The colorful peppers make a wonderful relish, either hot or cold.

1 cup extra-virgin olive oil

1 cup fresh oregano leaves

¼ cup fresh parsley leaves

5 cloves garlic

1 teaspoon grated lemon zest

1 teaspoon freshly squeezed lemon juice

1 teaspoon crushed red pepper

Four 16-ounce bone-in thick-cut pork chops

1 medium red onion, cut into quarters with root end left intact

1 red bell pepper

1 yellow bell pepper

1 orange bell pepper

2 teaspoons salt

1½ teaspoons freshly ground black pepper

Fleur de sel, for garnish (optional)

1. Combine ¾ cup of the olive oil, oregano, parsley, garlic, lemon zest, lemon juice, and crushed red pepper in a food processor, and process for 1 minute, or until the mixture comes together to form a loose emulsion.

2. Place the pork chops in a resealable plastic bag, and pour half of the oregano mixture over the chops. Seal the bag and marinate the pork chops for at least 2 hours and up to 24 hours in the refrigerator. (The longer you marinate the chops, the better the flavor.) Reserve the remaining oregano mixture.

3. Preheat a grill to medium-high, and lightly oil the grate.

4. In a medium mixing bowl, toss the onion quarters and bell peppers with ½ teaspoon of the salt, ¼ teaspoon of the pepper, the remaining ¼ cup olive oil, and 1 tablespoon of the remaining oregano mixture. Transfer the onions and peppers to the grill. Cook the onions for 2½ minutes on each side. Cook the peppers for 3 to 4 minutes on each side, or until the skin begins to blister. Return the peppers and onions to the mixing bowl, cover it with plastic wrap, and allow them to steam for 5 minutes.

5. Once the onions have cooled slightly, remove the root ends and julienne the quarters. Remove the skin, stems, and seeds from the peppers, and julienne the peppers. In a medium bowl, combine the julienned peppers, julienned onions, ½ teaspoon of the salt, ¼ teaspoon of the pepper, and the remaining oregano mixture. Toss to combine.

6. Remove the pork chops from the marinade (discard the marinade), and season each one with ⅛ teaspoon salt and ⅛ teaspoon pepper per side. Place the chops on the grill and cook for 4 minutes. Rotate the chops 90 degrees and cook for 3 minutes longer. Then turn the chops over, lower the heat to medium, and cook for 6 to 8 minutes. Transfer the pork chops to a platter and let them rest for at least 5 minutes.

7. Sprinkle the pork chops with a little fleur de sel if desired, and serve with the onions and peppers.

4 servings

GRILLED MARINATED SKIRT STEAK WITH WILTED WATERCRESS

Just a few years ago my butcher, Leonard (and man, what a butcher!), turned me on to these marinated skirt steaks. Well, ever since then, I've been experimenting with this fabulous cut, trying out different marinades and cooking techniques. I really think that skirt steaks are best done on the grill. Talk about a treat.

8 cloves garlic, sliced in half lengthwise

1 tablespoon chopped fresh rosemary

1 tablespoon chopped fresh sage

1 tablespoon chopped fresh thyme

3/4 cup extra-virgin olive oil

1/2 cup sherry vinegar

One 1 3/4- to 2-pound skirt steak

1 tablespoon kosher salt

2 teaspoons freshly ground black pepper

2 tablespoons unsalted butter

2 teaspoons minced garlic

12 ounces or 12 cups fresh watercress, coarse stems removed, well rinsed, with water still clinging to the leaves

1/2 teaspoon salt

Pinch of freshly ground white pepper

Crusty bread, for serving

1. Combine the halved garlic cloves, rosemary, sage, and thyme in a food processor, and process until smooth. Add the olive oil and sherry vinegar, and process to combine.

2. Season the skirt steak with the kosher salt and black pepper. Place it in a resealable plastic bag and add the garlic-herb marinade. Seal the bag, and refrigerate for at least 2 and up to 4 hours, turning occasionally.

3. Preheat a grill to medium-high.

4. Remove the steak from the refrigerator and allow it to come to room temperature for 30 minutes.

5. Remove the steak from the marinade (discard the marinade), and wipe any excess marinade off the steak with paper towels. Place the steak on the grill, and cook for 4 minutes. Rotate the steak 45 degrees and cook for another 4 minutes. Turn the steak over and cook for 4 to 6 minutes for medium-rare. Transfer the steak to a cutting board and let it rest for 5 to 7 minutes before slicing.

6. While the steak is resting, prepare the watercress: Set a large 12-inch skillet over medium-high heat and melt the butter in it. Add the minced garlic and cook, stirring, until it is soft and fragrant, about 1 minute. Add the watercress, ½ teaspoon of the salt, and the white pepper. Cook, stirring, until the watercress is wilted and tender, 3 to 4 minutes. Remove the skillet from the heat.

7. When ready to serve, thinly slice the steak across the grain. Serve it with crusty bread and the wilted watercress.

4 servings

SKIRT STEAK MARINATED ASIAN-STYLE

This simple Asian marinade also works wonders on chicken, seafood, and pork. Versatile and almost effortless, it will become a staple in your grilling repertoire.

1/4 cup soy sauce

2 tablespoons rice vinegar

2 tablespoons chopped green onions, white and green parts plus more for garnish

1 tablespoon chili oil

1 tablespoon dark Asian sesame oil

1 tablespoon chopped garlic

1 tablespoon minced fresh ginger

1 tablespoon minced lemongrass

Two 12-ounce skirt steaks

Cooked jasmine rice, for serving (optional)

1. Combine the soy sauce, vinegar, green onions, chili oil, sesame oil, garlic, ginger, and lemongrass in a bowl, and mix well. Pour the marinade into a large resealable plastic bag, and add the steaks. Squeeze the bag to remove excess air, and then seal it. Refrigerate for 24 hours, turning the bag occasionally.

2. Preheat a grill to high.

3. Remove the steaks from the marinade (discard the marinade), and blot them with paper towels to remove excess marinade. Place the steaks on the grill and cook until nicely marked on both sides, about 4 minutes on each side for medium-rare. Remove the steaks from the grill and let them rest for 10 minutes. Then thinly slice, and serve over jasmine rice if desired, garnished with chopped green onions.

4 servings

BABY LAMB CHOPS WITH MINT PESTO

These tiny chops make great party food—once they're frenched, the chops look like savory little lollipops. Love that!

12 single baby rib lamb chops (2 to 2½ pounds), frenched (see Note)

½ cup extra-virgin olive oil

2 tablespoons minced garlic

2 tablespoons minced fresh rosemary

2 tablespoons minced fresh mint

¼ cup freshly squeezed orange juice

2 teaspoons Emeril's Original Essence or Creole Seasoning (page 25)

1 teaspoon salt

1 teaspoon finely grated orange zest

½ teaspoon freshly ground black pepper

Mint Pesto (recipe follows), for serving

1. Place the lamb chops in a shallow nonreactive baking dish. In a bowl, combine the oil, garlic, rosemary, mint, orange juice, Original Essence, salt, orange zest, and pepper. Pour the marinade over the chops, and turn them to coat on both sides. Let sit at room temperature for 1 hour, or cover and refrigerate for up to 4 hours.

2. Preheat a grill to medium-high.

3. Place the lamb chops on the grill and cook for 2 to 3 minutes per side for medium-rare. Remove the chops from the grill, and serve with the Mint Pesto.

Note: To french a piece of meat is to cut or scrape the meat away from the end of a rib or chop, leaving the bone exposed.

4 servings

Mint Pesto

2 1/2 cups packed fresh mint leaves
1/4 cup grated Parmesan cheese
2 1/2 tablespoons pine nuts, toasted
1 to 2 cloves garlic, minced
1/2 cup extra-virgin olive oil
1/4 teaspoon salt
1/8 teaspoon freshly ground black pepper

Rinse the mint leaves well, and pat dry. Place the leaves in a blender and add the cheese, pine nuts, and garlic. Press the leaves down into the base of the blender, and cover the blender. Turn the blender on low speed, and slowly drizzle the olive oil through the feed tube; pulse the blender until combined. (Try not to over-purée; the sauce should be chunky-smooth.) Season with the salt and pepper, and pulse briefly to combine. Use immediately or cover with a thin film of oil and refrigerate for up to 2 days. **1 cup**

HANGER STEAK WITH A SMOKY PAPRIKA RUB

Did you know that there are many different types of paprika? It can be spicy or sweet, hot or mild. And then there's the smoked variety. Oh, man, talk about rich, deep flavor. Try to find Pimentón de la Vera—it's the real deal, straight from Spain, and you can usually find it in gourmet markets if not in the spice aisle of your local grocery store. It is smoked and can be either *dulce* (sweet) or *picante* (hot), and its flavor is like no other paprika.

2 pounds hanger steak, membrane trimmed

½ cup vegetable oil

½ cup balsamic vinegar

¼ cup sherry vinegar

½ cup apple juice

1½ cups chopped onions

¼ cup chopped garlic

2 tablespoons Smoky Paprika Rub (recipe follows), plus more for seasoning

1. Place the steak in a gallon-size resealable plastic bag.

2. Combine the oil, vinegars, apple juice, onions, garlic, and the 2 tablespoons Smoky Paprika Rub in a bowl, and stir well. Pour the mixture over the steak and seal the bag. Marinate in the refrigerator for 6 hours or up to overnight, turning the bag every few hours.

3. Remove the steak from the refrigerator 1 hour before cooking so it can come to room temperature.

4. Preheat a grill to high.

5. Remove the steak from the marinade (discard the marinade), and season it on both sides with Smoky Paprika Rub. Place the steak on the grill and cook for 2 minutes. Rotate the steak 90 degrees (for grill cross-hatch marks) and cook for another 2 minutes. Then turn the steak over and repeat, cooking it for about 4 minutes. (To avoid toughness, serve hanger steak rare to medium-rare.)

6. Let the steak rest for 5 minutes before slicing it against the grain and serving.

4 servings

Smoky Paprika Rub

3 tablespoons hot pimentón (smoked Spanish paprika), preferably Pimentón de la Vera picante
3 tablespoons salt
4 teaspoons granulated onion powder
2 teaspoons granulated garlic powder
2 teaspoons freshly ground white pepper
1 1/2 teaspoons freshly ground black pepper
1/4 teaspoon dried thyme
1/4 teaspoon dried oregano

Combine all the ingredients in a small mixing
bowl, and blend well. Store in an airtight container in a cool, dry, dark place for up to 3 months.

Generous 1/2 cup

Sweet

ENDINGS

ROOT BEER FLOATS

Remember these? Grab a frosty mug or an old-fashioned soda fountain glass.

1 liter root beer

4 large scoops vanilla ice cream

Flavored syrups, such as vanilla or
cherry

Crushed root beer candies, for
garnish

Fill four tall glasses three-quarters of the way with root beer. (You may want to set the glasses on small plates to catch any overflow from the fizz.) Place 1 scoop of vanilla ice cream in each glass. Top with a drizzle of your choice of flavored syrup. Sprinkle the crushed root beer candies over the top, and serve immediately, with long straws and long-handled spoons.

4 large floats

GRILLED CHOCOLATE SANDWICHES

Whip up a batch of these no-fuss delicious sandwiches for a quick and easy dessert.

Twelve ½-inch-thick slices challah, brioche, or pound cake

3 tablespoons Bing cherry preserves

Two 4-ounce good-quality bittersweet chocolate bars, each cut into thirds

⅓ cup unsalted butter, melted

Confectioners' sugar, for garnish

1. Preheat a grill, griddle, or nonstick grill pan to medium-low.

2. Lay the bread or cake slices on a work surface. Brush each of 6 slices with ½ tablespoon of the Bing cherry preserves. Top each brushed slice with 1 piece of the chocolate. Top with the remaining bread or cake slices. Brush the melted butter on both sides of each sandwich, and grill the sandwiches until the chocolate has melted and the bread is crisp and golden brown, 2 to 4 minutes per side. Cut the sandwiches in half or in quarters, dust with confectioners' sugar, and serve warm.

6 sandwiches

MINT JULEP SORBET

The mint julep is a Southern classic, particularly enjoyed in a chilled silver julep cup on Kentucky Derby day. This frozen version is sure to be a knockout.

1 cup sugar

2 cups water

1/2 cup packed fresh mint leaves

1/4 cup bourbon

1/4 cup club soda

Fresh mint sprigs,
    for garnish

1. Combine the sugar, water, and mint leaves in a small saucepan and bring to a boil, stirring to dissolve the sugar. Remove from the heat and set aside until cooled to room temperature.

2. Strain the cooled mint syrup through a fine-mesh sieve into a bowl; discard the solids. Add the bourbon and club soda to the strained syrup, stirring until combined. Freeze the mixture in an ice cream maker according to the manufacturer's directions.

3. Place the sorbet in a freezer-safe container and freeze it for 4 hours before serving.

4. Serve garnished with fresh mint sprigs.

4 to 6 servings

MANGO-BASIL FREEZE POPS

This is a great dessert to make for children—as well as those just young at heart. It will be the hit of your next grilling party.

1 cup sugar

1 cup water

1/2 cup packed fresh basil leaves, coarsely chopped

2 ripe mangoes, peeled, seeded, and cubed (about 2 1/2 cups)

1. Place the sugar and water in a small saucepan and bring to a boil, stirring to dissolve the sugar. Add the basil, cover, and remove from the heat. Let sit for 15 minutes. Then strain the syrup into a bowl (discard the basil leaves), and refrigerate until well chilled, 1 to 2 hours.

2. When the syrup has chilled, place the cubed mango in a food processor or blender and puree, adding the syrup little by little until it is fully incorporated and the fruit mixture is very smooth. Divide the fruit puree among six or eight 5-ounce paper cups, or better yet, among ice cube trays or Popsicle molds. Stand an ice cream stick or a small plastic spoon in the center of each cup.

3. Cut out six or eight 4-inch squares of aluminum foil. Poke a small hole in the center of each square, and place one square over each cup, pushing the stick or spoon handle through the hole to hold it in a straight upright position.

4. Stand the cups in the freezer and freeze until set, at least 8 hours or overnight.

5. Remove the pops from the freezer and discard the foil squares. Gently tear the paper cups away from the fruit pops, and serve.

6 to 8 freeze pops

GRILLED S'MORES

Sticky, gooey campfire treats right in your own backyard—they'll leave your guests screaming out for more!

4 large marshmallows, halved

4 to 8 pieces of milk chocolate candy bar squares

4 graham crackers, halved

1. Preheat a grill to low, and line half of the grate with aluminum foil.

2. String the marshmallow halves onto a long metal skewer.

3. Place 1 or 2 chocolate squares on 4 of the graham cracker halves. Arrange all of the graham cracker halves on the aluminum foil, and grill until they are toasted and the chocolate is soft, 1 to 2 minutes. Meanwhile, cook the marshmallows by constantly rotating the skewer over the open area of the grill until they turn light brown, develop a crust, and soften, 1 to 2 minutes. When the marshmallows are done, arrange them on the plain graham cracker halves. Immediately remove the graham crackers from the grill and sandwich them together. Serve immediately.

4 servings

GRILLED PEACHES WITH MASCARPONE AND HONEY

This is a simple but delicious dessert to make when peaches are at their best in the heart of summer. If you like, you can use vanilla ice cream in place of the mascarpone.

6 large ripe peaches, halved, and pitted

6 tablespoons honey, plus more for serving (optional)

8 ounces mascarpone cheese, at room temperature

1. Preheat a grill to medium-high.

2. Place the peaches, cut side down, on the grill and cook until lightly charred, 2 to 3 minutes. Transfer the peaches, cut side up, to a grill-proof baking dish or baking sheet, and drizzle them evenly with the honey. Place the dish on the grill and close the grill. Cook until the peaches are soft, about 5 minutes.

3. Remove the baking dish from the grill, and divide the peach halves among six dessert plates. Divide the mascarpone evenly among the plates, and drizzle with additional honey if desired. Serve immediately.

6 servings

GRILLED BANANA SPLITS WITH HOT FUDGE AND RUM CARAMEL SAUCE

Everyone loves banana splits. But, hey, when the bananas are grilled to caramelized perfection and then topped with goodies—watch out!

6 firm-ripe unpeeled bananas, halved lengthwise

6 tablespoons honey

12 tablespoons (3/4 cup) packed light brown sugar

Vanilla ice cream, for serving

Hot Fudge Sauce (recipe follows), for serving

Rum Caramel Sauce (recipe follows), for serving

2 cups lightly sweetened whipped cream, for serving

Finely chopped roasted lightly salted peanuts, for serving

6 maraschino cherries, for serving

1. Preheat a grill to high, and lightly oil the grill grate.

2. Place the banana halves, cut side up, on a baking sheet and drizzle the honey evenly over them. Sprinkle with the brown sugar. Place the bananas, cut side up, directly on the grill, arranging them so they are perpendicular to the grill grate. Close the grill cover and cook until the bananas are caramelized around the edges and the fruit is beginning to pull away from the peel, 3 to 5 minutes.

3. Carefully transfer the grilled banana halves (still in their skins) to a small baking sheet. Using two small forks or a long, thin spatula, carefully remove the banana halves from their skins and place 2 pieces of banana on each dessert plate. (This is a little tricky because the bananas are now very soft.) Top each banana with 1 or 2 scoops of vanilla ice cream. Drizzle with the Hot Fudge Sauce and Rum Caramel Sauce. Top with dollops of whipped cream and sprinkle with chopped peanuts. Garnish each banana split with a maraschino cherry, and serve immediately.

6 servings

Hot Fudge Sauce

$^1/_2$ cup sugar
$^1/_4$ cup unsweetened cocoa powder
$^3/_4$ cup heavy cream
$^1/_4$ cup plus 2 tablespoons light corn syrup
3 ounces semisweet chocolate, chopped
2 tablespoons unsalted butter
1 teaspoon vanilla extract
Pinch of salt

Combine the sugar and cocoa powder in the top of a double boiler set over briskly simmering water, and whisk to combine. Add the heavy cream and corn syrup, and whisk until smooth. Cook, whisking constantly, until the mixture is hot, thick, and creamy, 3 to 5 minutes. Add the chocolate, butter,

vanilla, and salt, and stir to combine. Cook, stirring occasionally, until the chocolate and butter are melted and the sauce is smooth, 2 to 3 minutes. Keep warm until ready to serve. (The sauce can be prepared up to several weeks in advance and reheated gently in a double boiler before serving.) Store it in a nonreactive airtight container, refrigerated. About 2 cups

Rum Caramel Sauce

3/4 cup sugar
1/4 cup hot water
1 cup plus 1 tablespoon heavy cream
2 tablespoons dark rum
1 teaspoon vanilla extract
2 teaspoons cold unsalted butter

1. Combine the sugar and hot water in a heavy saucepan, and cook over high heat until the sugar has dissolved, about 1 minute. Continue to cook, swirling the pan occasionally but never stirring the sugar mixture, until the mixture thickens and turns a deep amber color, 5 to 8 minutes. Remove the pan from the heat and immediately add the heavy cream (be careful—the mixture will splatter). Return the pan to the heat and reduce the heat to medium. Cook until the sauce is thick and creamy, stirring occasionally to help incorporate the cream, about 5 minutes.

2. Remove the pan from the heat and stir in the rum, vanilla, and butter. Serve warm. (If making the sauce in advance, rewarm gently before serving.) It will keep for several weeks refrigerated in an airtight container. About 1½ cups

RHODE ISLAND-STYLE FROZEN LEMONADE

Another childhood food memory is this frozen lemonade that you could buy from trucks along the beaches in coastal Rhode Island. Since those beaches were right around the corner from my childhood home in Fall River, Massachusetts, I must confess that I ate my fair share of these refreshing treats.

2 cups water

2½ cups sugar

2 cups freshly squeezed lemon juice

Candied Lemon Zest (recipe follows)

1. Combine the water and sugar in a small saucepan and heat just until the sugar has dissolved. Add the mixture to the lemon juice, and refrigerate until thoroughly chilled, 2 to 4 hours.

2. Freeze the lemonade in an ice cream machine according to the manufacturer's directions until it reaches a slushy consistency. Add the candied lemon zest. Serve with a straw and a spoon.

1 quart

Candied Lemon Zest

Blanching the lemon peel several times reduces the bitterness.

4 cups sugar, plus more for coating
2 cups water
Zest of 6 lemons, removed with a vegetable peeler, cut into small pieces

1. Bring the sugar and water to a boil in a 1-quart saucepan. Stir until the sugar has dissolved, and remove from the heat. Set aside.

2. Place the lemon zest in a separate saucepan, add cold water to cover, and bring to a boil. Drain the zest and rinse it under cold running water. Repeat this process two more times, using fresh water each time.

3. Place the blanched zest in a saucepan and add enough of the sugar syrup to cover it by 1 inch. Bring the syrup to a boil, and then reduce the heat to a simmer. Cook until the zest is tender and translucent, about 10 minutes. Remove the pan from the heat and let it cool. Then drain the zest. Lay the zest on a baking sheet to cool briefly. Then toss the zest in a shallow bowl of sugar until well coated. Transfer the candied zest to an airtight container and store it at room temperature for up to 1 month. **About 1 cup**

FRUIT KEBABS ON SUGARCANE SKEWERS WITH LIME HONEY

These are a lot of fun to make with the kids. They will enjoy putting them together, and everyone will enjoy eating them! If you can't find sugarcane sticks, you can simply use bamboo or metal skewers.

One 10-inch piece of sugarcane, cut into four 1/4-inch-thick sticks, or four 10-inch bamboo skewers soaked in warm water for 1 hour

1/4 pineapple, peeled, cored, and cut into eight 1-inch cubes (see page 238)

1 banana, peeled and cut into 8 equal portions

1 Gala, Fuji, or Red Delicious apple, cored and cut into 1-inch pieces

1 mango, peeled, pitted, and cut into eight 1-inch pieces

2 tablespoons honey

1/2 teaspoon grated lime zest

1. Thread each skewer with a cube of pineapple, banana, apple, and mango, and then repeat with the same fruit in the same sequence. Follow this procedure with the remaining three skewers.

2. Combine the honey and lime zest in a small bowl, and set aside until ready to use.

3. Preheat a grill to medium.

4. Place the kebabs on the grill and cook until the fruit is lightly charred on the first side, about 3 minutes. Turn the kebabs over and cook for another 3 minutes, brushing them with half of the lime honey. Turn them over again and cook for 1 minute while brushing with the remainder of the lime honey. Turn once more and cook for 1 minute longer.

5. Remove the skewers from the grill and serve immediately.

4 servings

ICE CREAM SANDWICHES

Chewy oatmeal banana cookies combined with caramel ice cream make this dessert an all-time favorite. But just about any flavor of ice cream will go with these chewy cookies. The kids will enjoy decorating them, too!

1¾ cups quick-cooking rolled oats

1½ cups all-purpose flour

2 teaspoons baking powder

½ teaspoon salt

¼ teaspoon baking soda

6 tablespoons (¾ stick) unsalted butter, at room temperature

2 tablespoons creamy peanut butter

1 cup firmly packed light brown sugar

½ cup granulated sugar

2 teaspoons vanilla extract

1 large egg

1 very ripe banana, peeled and cut into small pieces

Caramel ice cream or vanilla frozen yogurt, or your favorite flavor of frozen yogurt

Chopped nuts, chocolate-covered candies, jimmies, sprinkles, etc., as desired, for rolling and decorating (optional)

1. Position the oven rack in the center of the oven and preheat the oven to 350°F.

2. Combine the rolled oats, flour, baking powder, salt, and baking soda in a medium mixing bowl, and stir well. Set aside.

3. Place the butter, peanut butter, light brown sugar, and granulated sugar in the bowl of an electric mixer and cream the ingredients on high speed. Add the vanilla and egg, and mix on medium speed. Add the banana and mix until it has been almost completely incorporated. Stop the mixer and scrape down the sides of the bowl with a rubber spatula. Add the oat mixture and combine on low speed.

4. Form the dough into balls, using about 2 table-spoonfuls for each. Divide the balls of dough among three large ungreased baking sheets, spacing them about 2 inches apart, and press to slightly flatten them (about 8 cookies per baking sheet). Bake, in batches, until they are golden around the edges, about 11 minutes. Remove the cookies from the oven and allow them to cool for 2 minutes on the baking sheets. Then transfer them to wire racks to cool completely. You will need 12 cookies for the ice cream sandwiches. Extra cookies can be stored in an airtight container or enjoyed immediately.

5. To build the ice cream sandwiches, soften the ice cream or frozen yogurt by setting it aside at room temperature for 15 minutes. Line a baking sheet with parchment or waxed paper.

6. Using a small (tablespoon-size) ice cream scoop, place 3 or 4 scoops of ice cream on the bottom side of one cookie. Working quickly, top it with a second cookie and press lightly to push the ice cream to the edges of the cookie. Use a small spatula to smooth the ice cream around the edges of the sandwich. If using, place chopped nuts or your decorations of choice in a shallow container, and roll the edges of the ice cream sandwich in the nuts, pressing lightly to coat. Repeat, placing the ice cream sandwiches on the prepared baking sheet as they are made and freezing them immediately until firm, about 2 hours.

6 large ice cream sandwiches

COCONUT LAYER CAKE

If you bring this to a grilling party, I'm telling you, you will be the smash, the bomb, the top *dawg* of the neighborhood. This cake is absolutely fantastic— even a little bit sinful.

Nonstick cooking spray

4½ cups cake flour, plus more for dusting the pans

2 tablespoons baking powder

½ teaspoon salt

11 ounces (2¾ sticks) unsalted butter, at room temperature

2¼ cups sugar

1½ cups unsweetened coconut milk (see Notes)

7 egg whites (9 ounces) (reserve 4 yolks for the filling)

1 tablespoon vanilla extract

⅓ cup Cruzan coconut rum (see Notes) (optional)

Coconut Cream Filling (recipe follows)

Coconut Frosting (recipe follows)

3 cups sweetened flaked coconut, toasted, for garnish

1. Preheat the oven to 350°F. Grease three 10-inch round cake pans with nonstick cooking spray. Cut three circles of parchment paper to fit the bottom of the cake pans. Line the bottom of the pans with the parchment, then grease the parchment with nonstick cooking spray, and then lightly dust the parchment and the sides of the pans with flour.

2. Sift the flour, baking powder, and salt together into a large bowl.

3. In a standing electric mixer, cream the butter and sugar on low speed until light and fluffy.

4. In a separate bowl, whisk the coconut milk, egg whites, and vanilla together. With the electric mixer still on low speed, begin alternately adding the liquid and the dry ingredients to the creamed butter in three stages, beginning with the liquid and mixing well after each addition (to minimize mess when adding flour, add just a bit at a time). Divide the batter evenly among the prepared cake pans. Tap the pans lightly on the counter to eliminate any air bubbles, and place them in the oven. Bake for 25 minutes, or until the cake pulls away from the sides of the pans and a toothpick inserted into the center comes out clean. Let the cakes cool in the pans for 10 minutes, and then turn them out onto wire cooling racks to cool completely. Brush the cooled layers with the coconut rum, if desired.

5. To assemble the cake, place a cooled cake layer, bottom side up, on a serving plate, and spoon ¾ cup of the coconut filling onto the middle of the layer. Spread the filling evenly to within ¼ inch of the edge. Repeat with the second layer and another ¾ cup of filling. Stack the two filled layers on top of one another, and top with the final cake layer, top side up. Lightly frost the top and sides of the cake with some of the coconut frosting (this is called a crumb coating), and refrigerate the cake for 10 minutes. Then generously frost it again. Press the toasted coconut into the frosting on the top and sides of the cake. (This cake will keep for 2 days at room temperature.)

12 servings

Coconut Cream Filling

1 cup sweetened flaked coconut
4 egg yolks (reserve the whites for the cake batter)
½ cup sugar
⅛ teaspoon salt
8 tablespoons (1 stick) unsalted butter, at room temperature
¼ cup unsweetened coconut milk (see Notes)
¾ cup whole milk
1 teaspoon vanilla extract

1. Preheat the oven to 350°F.

2. Spread the coconut on a baking sheet and bake it, undisturbed, for 15 minutes. The color should range from dark brown to light. Set the toasted coconut aside.

3. Whisk the egg yolks, sugar, and salt together in a heavy-bottomed saucepan. Then whisk in the butter, coconut milk, milk, and vanilla. Cook over medium-low heat, stirring continuously with a heat-resistant rubber spatula or whisk, until thickened, taking care not to let it get so hot that the yolks scramble, about 10 minutes. The pastry cream will have a pudding-like consistency. Transfer it to a clean metal bowl set over an ice bath.

4. When the pastry cream has cooled, stir in the toasted coconut. Cover the surface directly with plastic wrap, and refrigerate until chilled, at least 3 hours or up to overnight. (It works best when chilled overnight.) **1½ cups**

Coconut Frosting

8 ounces (2 sticks) unsalted butter, at room temperature
8 cups confectioners' sugar, plus up to 1 cup more if needed
³/₄ cup whole milk
¹/₄ cup Cruzan coconut rum (see Notes) or milk
¹/₄ teaspoon salt
1 teaspoon vanilla extract

1. Place a small saucepan of water on the stove and heat to a simmer. Place the butter in the bowl of a standing electric mixer, and position the bowl on top of the saucepan. Once the butter has melted, remove the bowl from the heat and whisk in the 8 cups confectioners' sugar and the milk, rum, and salt. Place the bowl back on top of the simmering water and cook for 3 minutes, whisking occasionally (be sure not to cook longer than 3 minutes or the frosting will become grainy). Fit the electric mixer with the whisk attachment, and attach the bowl of frosting. Add the vanilla and whisk on medium speed for 15 minutes, or until cool.

2. Transfer the frosting to a container, cover it with plastic wrap, and set it aside until ready to use. Whisk it again right before frosting the cake. If the frosting seems too thin, whisk in up to 1 more cup of confectioners' sugar. **5 cups**

Notes: Coconut milk comes in 13.5-ounce and 14-ounce cans. This cake recipe is designed to use the entire can. If you come up a little short on the measurements asked for in the recipe, substitute whole milk.

This cake was made using Cruzan coconut rum. We found that the subtle, natural coconut flavor from this rum delightfully enhanced the cake and frosting. We recommend it highly.

CHOCOLATE CHIPOTLE BROWNIES

These super-fudgie brownies with a little chile kick are sure to get you fired up!

8 ounces (2 sticks) plus 1 teaspoon unsalted butter

1 cup plus 1 tablespoon all-purpose flour

4 ounces unsweetened chocolate, roughly chopped

1¹/₂ cups sugar

1 teaspoon ground cinnamon

³/₄ teaspoon chipotle powder

4 eggs, lightly beaten

1 cup chopped Mexican chocolate or semisweet chocolate morsels

1. Preheat the oven to 325°F. Grease an 11 X 7-inch baking dish with the 1 teaspoon butter, and dust it with the 1 tablespoon flour.

2. Combine the remaining 1 cup butter and the unsweetened chocolate in a saucepan, and warm over low heat, stirring constantly, until melted. Remove from the heat.

3. In a medium bowl, stir the remaining 1 cup flour with the sugar, cinnamon, and chipotle powder. Add the dry mixture to the melted chocolate mixture, stirring to combine. Add the eggs, mixing until smooth. Stir in the Mexican chocolate.

4. Pour the mixture into the prepared baking dish, and bake until the center is just set, 35 to 40 minutes. (Don't overbake, as these brownies are meant to be gooey.) Cool completely in the dish, and then cut into small squares.

About 24 brownies

PEPPERMINT ICE CREAM

This creamy, refreshing, peppermint-studded ice cream is not just for the holidays. It will make any occasion feel special.

4 cups half-and-half

1 vanilla bean, split, seeds scraped out and reserved

Pinch of salt

1 cup sugar

8 egg yolks

½ cup packed fresh mint leaves

½ cup crushed peppermint candies

1. Combine the half-and-half, the vanilla bean and seeds, and the salt in a nonreactive saucepan and place it over medium heat. Bring just to a boil, and then immediately remove the pan from the heat.

2. Beat the sugar and egg yolks together in a bowl. Gradually add the half-and-half mixture, about ¼ cup at a time, to the beaten eggs, whisking between additions, until completely combined. Pour the mixture back into the saucepan and add the mint leaves. Cook over medium-low heat, stirring, until the mixture thickens enough to coat the back of a spoon, 5 to 6 minutes. Remove from the heat, strain through a fine-mesh sieve into a bowl, and cool completely. Then transfer the custard, covered, to the refrigerator and chill it thoroughly, about 2 hours.

3. Pour the chilled custard into an ice cream machine and follow the manufacturer's instructions. As the ice cream begins to set, sprinkle the crushed peppermint candies into it while it continues to churn. Remove the ice cream from the machine, place it in a freezer-safe container, and freeze until firm, about 8 hours.

6 cups

FRESH STRAWBERRY PIE

This old-fashioned favorite comes to me by way of my friend Kamili's mom, Gwendolyn, who lives in Jackson, Mississippi. And, boy, let me tell you, she has a good thing going with this one. In her own words, "It's a showstopper!" Don't hesitate to make this pie a day or two in advance, and then just pull it out of the fridge when you are ready to enjoy it. Thanks, Gwen!

2 pounds fresh strawberries, rinsed and hulled

1/2 cup plus 2 tablespoons sugar

2 1/2 teaspoons cornstarch

1 1/2 teaspoons freshly squeezed lemon juice

1/8 teaspoon salt

2 1/2 teaspoons unflavored powdered gelatin

2 tablespoons cold water

1 baked Flaky Pie Crust (recipe follows)

1 cup cold heavy whipping cream

1/4 cup warm water

1/2 teaspoon vanilla extract

1. Slice about 3 cups of the strawberries 1/4 inch thick, and place them in a medium bowl. Crush the sliced berries with a potato masher or a fork; you should have about 1 1/2 cups crushed berries. Place them in a small saucepan. Add the 1/2 cup sugar and the cornstarch, lemon juice, and salt, and stir to combine.

2. Soften 1 1/2 teaspoons of the gelatin in the cold water, and set it aside.

3. Place the saucepan over low heat and bring the berry mixture to a simmer. Cook, stirring occasionally, until the mixture is transparent and of medium thickness, about 5 minutes. Remove from the heat, add the softened gelatin, and stir until the gelatin has dissolved. Set aside to cool.

4. Cut 1 cup of the remaining berries into quarters, and gently fold them into the cooled cooked mixture. Pour the filling into the baked pie shell, and chill in the refrigerator until set, at least 1 hour, and up to overnight before serving.

5. Chill the whisk attachment and the bowl of an electric mixer in the refrigerator for about 10 minutes.

6. Attach the bowl and whisk to the mixer, and add the heavy cream and the remaining 2 tablespoons sugar. Whip until soft peaks form.

7. Soften the remaining 1 teaspoon gelatin in the warm water, and set aside until cool but not set. With the mixer running, add the softened gelatin to the whipped cream and whip until stiff peaks form. Add the vanilla. Working quickly, use a spatula to top the pie with the whipped cream, spreading it evenly and smoothly. Return the pie to the refrigerator and chill until set, at least 45 minutes.

8. Slice or halve the remaining strawberries, and arrange them decoratively on top of the pie. (The pie will keep for up to 3 days in the refrigerator.)

6 to 8 servings

Flaky Pie Crust

1⅓ cups flour, sifted, plus more for dusting
⅛ teaspoon salt
8 tablespoons (1 stick) cold unsalted butter,
    cut into ¼-inch dice
4 to 5 tablespoons ice water

1. Combine the flour and salt in a medium mixing bowl. Add the butter and cut it into the flour with a pastry blender, fork, or your fingers until the mixture resembles coarse crumbs. Sprinkle in 4 tablespoons of the ice water while continuing to blend. Press the dough into a ball, and work it with your hands until the mixture just comes together, adding up to 1 tablespoon more ice water if needed. Flatten it into a disk and wrap it in plastic wrap. Chill the dough in the refrigerator for at least 1 hour and up to 2 days. (The dough can also be frozen and then thawed in the refrigerator before using.)

2. Preheat the oven to 450°F.

3. Remove the dough from the refrigerator and allow it to soften slightly, about 10 minutes. Lightly dust a clean work surface with flour, and roll the dough into a 12-inch round, about ⅛ inch thick. Fit the pastry loosely into a 9- or 10-inch pie pan. Trim and flute the edge. Prick the bottom of the pie shell thoroughly with a fork, line it with parchment paper, and then weight it with ceramic or metal pie weights. Bake for 12 minutes. Remove the parchment and weights, and continue to bake until the crust is lightly golden and cooked through, about 7 minutes longer.

4. Allow the pie shell to cool completely before filling. **One 9- or 10-inch pie shell**

BLUEBERRY CORNMEAL SHORTCAKES

Everybody loves strawberry shortcake, but when they're in season in the summertime, there is nothing like local blueberries. Here they are macerated with just a tiny bit of sugar and a hint of Grand Marnier. The addition of cornmeal to the shortcakes is an unexpectedly delicious twist on the classic.

1 quart fresh blueberries, rinsed, stemmed, and picked over

10 tablespoons plus 1½ teaspoons sugar

¼ cup Grand Marnier

1½ cups all-purpose flour, plus more for kneading

¼ cup plus 2 tablespoons yellow cornmeal

¾ teaspoon baking powder

½ teaspoon baking soda

¼ teaspoon salt

1 egg

¼ cup plus 2 tablespoons buttermilk

7 tablespoons cold unsalted butter, cut into ½-inch pieces

¾ cup cold heavy whipping cream

1. Using a fork, mash 1 cup of the blueberries in a medium bowl. Add the remaining whole blueberries, 6 tablespoons of the sugar, and the Grand Marnier, and stir to combine. Cover the bowl with plastic wrap and let it sit at room temperature for at least 2 hours and up to overnight, stirring the berries intermittently, until they are sweetened and have released some of their juices.

2. Position an oven rack in the upper third of the oven, and preheat the oven to 450°F.

3. Sift the flour, cornmeal, baking powder, baking soda, salt, and 3 tablespoons of the remaining sugar into a medium mixing bowl. In a small bowl, whisk together the egg and ¼ cup buttermilk.

4. Using your hands or a pastry blender, cut the butter into the flour mixture until the mixture resembles very coarse crumbs. Make a well in the dry ingredients and add the buttermilk mixture. Stir with a rubber spatula until just combined. Transfer the dough to a lightly floured surface, and knead it with floured hands ten times, or until the dough just comes together and is smooth. Gently roll out the dough to ½-inch thickness. Using a 3-inch round cutter dipped in flour, cut out 3 biscuits and place them on an ungreased baking sheet. Gather the dough scraps, re-form the dough, roll it out, and repeat. Brush the biscuits lightly with the remaining 2 tablespoons buttermilk, and sprinkle the tops with the 1½ teaspoons sugar. Bake for 5 minutes. Then rotate the baking sheet and bake until the biscuits are golden and a tester inserted into the center of one comes out clean, about 5 minutes. Transfer the biscuits to a wire rack to cool.

5. Put the remaining 1 tablespoon sugar in a medium bowl, add the heavy cream, and whisk until the cream is thickened and just stiff, about 3 minutes. Refrigerate until ready to use.

6. To assemble the shortcakes: Halve each biscuit and place the bottom halves on six dessert plates. Spoon ½ cup of the macerated berries onto each half. Spoon a generous dollop of the whipped cream over the berries, and top with the other biscuit half. Serve immediately.

Note: If you like, grill the halved biscuits, cut side down, for 30 to 60 seconds on a hot grill to crisp them slightly before assembling the desserts.

6 servings

CHOCOLATE-STUFFED APPLES ON THE GRILL

This idea came to me years back from a friend in Tennessee who is a grillmaster. Boy, am I ever thankful. I've been making these ever since, and am glad to share them with you.

6 Braeburn, Honeycrisp, or Jonagold apples

12 "fun size" Snickers bars (1/2 ounce each), roughly chopped

3 tablespoons unsalted butter

3/4 cup apple juice

1 1/2 tablespoons sugar

Vanilla ice cream, for serving (optional)

1. Preheat a grill to medium-low.

2. Using a sharp knife, carefully cut the top 1/2 inch from each apple. Using an apple corer or a small melon baller, scoop out the stem, core, and seeds from each apple, leaving the bottom intact. Fill each apple with about 2 tablespoons of the chopped Snickers, and top each apple with 1 1/2 teaspoons of the butter.

3. Combine the apple juice and sugar in a measuring cup, and stir until the sugar has dissolved. Place each apple on a piece of aluminum foil, and pull the sides up (so the apple juice mixture will not leak out). Spoon 3 tablespoons of the apple juice mixture over each apple, bring the foil edges together, and seal the foil packets tightly.

4. Place the apples on the grill, close the lid, and cook until tender, 15 to 20 minutes. Let the packets rest briefly, and then carefully open them. Transfer the apples to shallow bowls. Pour any accumulated juices over the apples and serve hot, with a scoop of vanilla ice cream if desired.

6 servings

GRILLED PINEAPPLE "SUZETTE"

Inspired by the classic Crêpes Suzette . . . but adapted for the grill and done without crêpes! I've found that pineapple, a wonderful fruit that is available nearly year-round, works great on the grill, whether sliced or in wedges. If you don't want to fuss with the sauce, simple grilled slices stand on their own with a scoop of vanilla ice cream.

1 firm-ripe pineapple

4 teaspoons unsalted butter

1/4 cup sugar

Juice of 1 lime

1/4 cup pineapple-flavored rum, preferably Cruzan brand

1/4 cup pineapple juice

1 tablespoon finely chopped fresh mint, for garnish

Vanilla ice cream, for serving (optional)

1. Remove the top of the pineapple by holding it firmly and twisting it off. Use a sharp serrated knife to trim off both ends of the pineapple. Set the pineapple upright on a cutting board, and starting at the top, cut the skin off by following the curve of the fruit with a sharp knife. Overlap your cuts to ensure that you cut out all the eyes (the brown indentations on the pineapple).

2. Once all of the skin has been removed, slice the pineapple in half from the top down. Slice each half in half again, from the top down. Slice each quarter lengthwise into 3 equal wedges. Use your knife to cut the core out of each wedge, so that you have a total of 12 trapezoidal wedges.

3. Set 8 wedges aside. Cut the remaining 4 wedges into 1/4-inch cubes. You should have about 1 cup diced pineapple.

4. Preheat a grill to medium-high, and oil the grate.

5. Lay the pineapple wedges on the grill and cook for 2 to 2 1/2 minutes. Rotate the wedges 90 degrees, and cook for another 2 to 2 1/2 minutes. Turn them onto the second side and cook for 2 to 2 1/2 minutes. Turn them onto the third side and cook for a final 2 to 2 1/2 minutes. Transfer the grilled pineapple to a platter, arranging it with the crosshatched sides facing up.

6. While the pineapple is grilling, set a 10-inch grill-proof sauté pan on the grill and add 2 teaspoons of the butter. Once the butter melts, add the diced pineapple and sauté, stirring it occasionally, for 5 minutes. Add the sugar and cook until the sugar dissolves, starts to form large bubbles, and turns golden, 6 to 8 minutes. Add the lime juice and swirl the pan to incorporate it. Cook for 3 minutes. Then add the rum to the pan, and cook for 3 minutes. Then add the pineapple juice and continue to cook until the liquid has reduced by half, 4 to 5 minutes. Remove the pan from the heat and swirl the remaining 2 teaspoons butter into the sauce.

7. Pour the hot sauce over the grilled pineapple, and garnish with the chopped mint. Serve with a scoop of vanilla ice cream, if desired.

4 to 6 servings